50

American Serial Killers You've Probably Never Heard Of

Volume Five

Robert Keller

**Please Leave Your Review of This Book At
http://bit.ly/kellerbooks**

ISBN-13: 978-1535138468

ISBN-10: 1535138467

© 2016 by Robert Keller

robertkellerauthor.com

Table of Contents

Lowell Amos

In December 1994, a group of executives was gathered at the Atheneum Hotel in Detroit for a company Christmas party. Among their number was Lowell Amos, a 52-year-old GM plant manager from Anderson, Indiana. Accompanying Amos was his wife, Roberta. The couple partied late into the night, eventually retiring at 4:30 a.m.

At around 8:30, GM executive, Norbert Crabtree, received a frantic phone call from Lowell Amos. Crabtree and another guest, Daniel Porcasi, went to Amos's room, where he told them that his wife had died in a tragic accident. He begged for their help in cleaning up the scene and eventually convinced Crabtree to hold onto his sports coat and a small leather case. When Crabtree later checked inside the case, he found it to contain a syringe without a needle.

With the scene cleaned up, Amos called the police. When they arrived he told them that Roberta had overdosed during a cocaine-fueled sex game. She couldn't snort the drug due to a sinus problem, he said, so she diluted it in water and injected it into her vagina. She'd still been taking cocaine when he fell asleep. When he awoke, she was dead.

The story sounded highly suspicious, especially as it was obvious that Amos had cleaned up the room and washed his wife's body before calling the cops. Other parts of the story didn't add up either. A person overdosing on cocaine would thrash violently in their death throes. How was it possible that Amos had slept through it? How had he fallen asleep at all, given the amount of cocaine he claimed to have taken? Then there was the makeup smeared on a pillowcase. Evidence perhaps that Roberta had been suffocated?

Despite these, and other suspicious details, there wasn't enough to charge Amos with murder. Nonetheless, investigators decided to keep him under surveillance while they firmed up their case. He hardly acted like the grieving widow. Two days after Roberta's death he spent $1,000 on dinner and drinks with two women and had sex with both of them.

Meanwhile, the death of Roberta Amos had been widely reported in the media. In the wake of the coverage, the police began receiving calls from former lovers of Lowell Amos. Several of them complained that he'd drugged them during sex. These accusations convinced investigators to look into Lowell Amos's past. What they found, shocked them.

His first wife, Saundra had been found dead in the bathroom of their home in 1979. According to Amos, she had mixed wine and sedatives and had fallen and hit her head on the side of the tub. The cause of death was ruled indeterminate, and Amos received a $350,000 insurance payout.

Within months of Saundra's death, Amos married his long-time mistress, Caroline. However, when the new Mrs. Amos learned that he had taken out a large policy on her life, she threw him out.

Amos moved in next with his 76-year-old mother. A few weeks later, the old woman was dead. Although she'd previously been in good health, no autopsy was called for. Amos inherited more than $1 million.

Shortly after, Amos and Caroline were reconciled and he moved back in. Perhaps she believed that his newfound fortune would insulate her from any plans he may have been brewing beforehand. She was wrong.

Within nine months, she too was dead. According to Amos, she'd been blow-drying her hair in the bathroom. Later he found her in the tub and thought she might have been electrocuted. Caroline's death netted Amos another $800,000 insurance payment.

The pattern was too much of a coincidence and on November 8, 1998, Lowell Amos was arrested for the murder of his third wife, Roberta.

Although he was never charged with the murders of Saundra, Caroline, and his mother, Michigan law allowed details of these crimes to be entered into the record, in order to establish a pattern.

This testimony, together with the crime scene evidence and a clear motive (it turned out that Roberta was preparing to leave him), made a strong case.

Lowell Amos was found guilty of murder on October 24, 1996. He was sentenced to life imprisonment without possibility of parole.

Ralph Andrews

Illinois investigators called him a killing machine, who was worse than John Wayne Gacy. They also referred to him as a real-life Hannibal Lecter. And if Ralph Andrews is to be believed then those descriptors are apt. He claimed to have killed as many as 40 women, making him one of America's most prolific serial killers.

Andrews was already serving life at Statesville Correctional Center in Illinois when his boasts first reached the ears of the authorities. According to Andrews' cellmate, he claimed to have assaulted, murdered and eviscerated women across Illinois, Wisconsin, and Michigan.

Such boasts are of course commonplace among convicts hoping to make a name for themselves. But as Andrews was in prison for two murders bearing exactly those characteristics, the authorities took this information very seriously. They obtained a court order authorizing them to bug Andrews' cell. The information they gleaned was extremely interesting.

Investigators had long suspected Andrews in the 1977 rape and murder of 16-year-old Susan Clarke. Now here he was on tape, providing a detailed confession, describing how he'd abducted Susan as she walked home from a babysitting job, how he'd sexually assaulted her, then shot her in the head, how he'd sliced open her abdomen and then dumped her in a vegetable field near Eden's Expressway.

Armed with this information, Illinois authorities called in the help of famed FBI investigator, and one of the world's foremost authorities on serial killers, Robert Ressler.

Ressler's findings firmed up what many already suspected. He called Andrews a model serial killer. "No one I've seen of late fits the pattern of a serial killer as strongly as he does," he concluded.

But did Andrews really kill as many as 40 women?

Ressler wasn't asked to speculate on the number, but he did state that of the cases he looked at, Andrews was likely responsible for at least five. These included;

Elizabeth West, a 14-year-old freshman at Belleville Township High. Elizabeth disappeared a block from her home as she was returning from a school play. Her strangled body was found in a creek between Belleville and Millstadt on May 5, 1978.

Ruth Ann Jany, 21, discovered in July 1979, five miles south of where Elizabeth West had been found. She had disappeared a year earlier after stopping at an ATM in downtown Belleville.

An unidentified woman, estimated to be between 18 and 23 years old, strangled near Summerfield in St. Clair County in September 1986. Her body was discovered in a cornfield.

Kristina Povolish, 19 years old. Her strangled corpse was found hidden in a ditch southwest of Belleville in July 1987.

Audrey Cardenas, a 24-year-old newspaper intern, whose badly decomposed body turned up in a creek on the campus of Belleville Township High School in June 1988.

Ralph Andrews was delighted to have such an esteemed investigator as Robert Ressler looking into his case. He agreed with Ressler that the five women had been killed by the same man, and even claimed that he knew who the killer was.

"Except it wasn't me," he said. "Because I haven't murdered anyone."

Such games are of course commonplace with serial killers, and in the absence of solid evidence, Andrews would never stand trial for the crimes. He died in prison of natural causes on January 31, 2006, taking his secrets to the grave.

Patrick Baxter

The murders had lain unsolved for over 12 years and there seemed to be very little hope of solving them. Sure there was DNA evidence, but the quantities lifted from the crime scenes were insufficient for a match. Then came yet another breakthrough in the application of this exemplary technology and suddenly the crimes were solvable.

But even as investigators rejoiced at the prospect of bringing the perpetrators to justice, they were in for a shock. The three murders – committed in disparate locations, by different methods, and against women of different races – were the work of the same man.

The first murder occurred on June 6, 1987. On that day, Michelle Walker, a ninth-grade student, was on her way to buy a pizza when she disappeared near her family's home on Warburton Avenue in Yonkers, New York. Her body was found the following day, concealed among some trees. She'd been sexually assaulted and then suffocated by someone who had covered her nose and mouth with his hand. Her jewelry was gone and she'd also been robbed of the cash she'd been carrying.

Seven months later, on New Year's Day, 1987, another Yonkers resident, Patricia England, was celebrating her 19th birthday.

Sometime during the day, Patricia told her family that she was going to visit a friend. She never made it.

It would be two months before police found Patricia's body near the Greenburgh-Yonkers border on February 6. An autopsy determined that she'd been sexually assaulted and had died of possible asphyxia. Date of death was set at around January 1, the day on which she'd disappeared. Investigators also believed that she'd been killed elsewhere, her body dumped where it had been found.

Initially, the investigation focused on a former boyfriend but he was quickly eliminated once it was determined that his blood type did not match the semen found at the scene.

On the morning of July 17, 1990, Lisa Gibbens left her apartment bound for a medical office in Hartsdale, where she'd recently started work as a receptionist. Lisa did not show up for work that day. Her body was found shortly after 9 a.m., hidden along the path she would have taken to the train station. Her purse and jewelry were missing, and there was evidence at the scene (later confirmed by an autopsy) that she'd been sexually assaulted. Cause of death was a gunshot wound to the back of the head, delivered by a sawn-off shotgun.

As in the England case, suspicion fell initially on the boyfriend, but he proved to have a cast iron alibi. Then a new suspect emerged. Douglas Steadman was the cousin of Westchester police commissioner, Anthony Mosca, and had been involved in a secret relationship with Lisa Gibbens. DNA testing cleared him of any involvement in the crime. The police were back to square one.

Unbeknownst to investigators, there was a man with links to at least one of the victims, and two of the crime scenes. Patrick Baxter lived along the stretch of road that Michelle Walker had disappeared from; he was known to hang out with friends at the Crestwood station where Lisa Gibbens was murdered; he had worked with Patricia England's former boyfriend and had met her. None of this came to light during the initial investigations.

Then in 2000, advances in DNA technology allowed the semen samples to be re-tested. They produced a match to a single perpetrator, Patrick Baxter.

Baxter, serving a term for car theft at the time, was charged with three counts of murder. He was found guilty and given a sentence of 75 years to life.

Larry Gene Bell

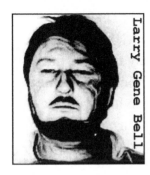

Larry Gene Bell was born on October 30, 1949, in Ralph, Alabama. His family was constantly on the move during his childhood and by the time he graduated high school in 1967, he'd lived in Alabama, South Carolina, and Mississippi. As a young adult, he settled in Columbia, South Carolina, where he married and fathered a son.

In 1970, he joined the Marines, but his military career lasted less than a year before he was discharged after accidently shooting himself in the knee. Returning to his hometown, Bell worked for a short time as a prison guard before moving his family to Rock Hill, South Carolina. In 1976, he and his wife divorced.

Bell's first known victim was Sandee Elaine Cornett, the girlfriend of a co-worker, who disappeared in Charlotte, North Carolina, in 1984. Cornett's body was never recovered and although there was evidence linking Bell to the crime, it was not enough to make a case for murder. Investigators were forced to let the matter drop.

Unfortunately, this would have tragic consequences for two young girls.

At around 3:15 p.m. on Friday, May 31, 1985, 17-year-old Sharon "Shari" Faye Smith arrived at her parents' home in Lexington County, South Carolina. Shari's father saw her park her car at the end of the long driveway and get out, presumably to check the mailbox. When the car was still standing there minutes later he went to investigate and found the vehicle unattended, with the engine still running. A frantic search of the area turned up no sign of his daughter and Bob Smith immediately called the police.

A massive search for Shari eventually turned up her body on June 5, 1985, but only after her abductor phoned the FBI to provide details of its location. In the intervening week, the abductor had carried out a sick campaign, constantly harassing the distraught parents with phone calls in which he described what he'd done to their daughter.

During this time, the Smiths also received a letter from Shari, apparently drafted under instruction of her kidnapper. Entitled "Last Will and Testament," it read in part, "I'll be with my Father now. Please do not become hard or upset. Everything works out for the good for those that love the Lord."

Following the discovery of Shari's body, Bell continued making taunting phone calls to the Smiths. Over the next three weeks, he callously described how he'd abducted Shari at gunpoint, raped and sodomized her, then wrapped duct tape around her head and suffocated her.

In one call, he provided details of another murder and gave directions to the location of the body. Ten-year-old Debra May Helmick had been kidnapped two weeks after Shari Smith.

But Bell's taunting of the Smith family would eventually come back to haunt him. Investigators were able to lift the imprint of a telephone number from the paper used to draft Shari's "Last Will & Testament." It led them directly to Bell. Evidence found in his house confirmed his involvement in Shari's murder, as well as that of Debra May Helmick.

Because of the excessive publicity surrounding the case, Bell's trial was moved to Moncks Corner, 100 miles from Columbia. He took the stand in his own defense and delivered six hours of bizarre testimony, during which he proclaimed himself to be Jesus Christ, and asked Dawn Smith (Shari's sister) to marry him.

If his intention was to launch an insanity defense, it failed. He was found guilty and sentenced to die. Larry Gene Bell was put to death in South Carolina's electric chair on October 4, 1996.

Rudy Bladel

The son of a Chicago railroad employee, Rudy Bladel developed an early love for trains and was determined to work on the railroad when he grew up. He got his first opportunity while serving with the US Air Force in Korea, where he was assigned to work on military supply trains. Returning to civilian life, he found work with his father's employer, the Rock Island and Pacific line, and settled in Niles, a suburb of Chicago.

In 1959, Rock Island and Pacific moved its base to Elkhart, Indiana, resulting in widespread layoffs. Bladel was one of those who lost his job and although he found employment with another rail company, he remained bitter about the circumstances of his dismissal. That bitterness would continue to fester and grow for three years. Eventually, it exploded into violence.

On August 3, 1963, two rail employees, engineer Roy Bottorf, and fireman Paul Overstreet, were found dead in the cab of their train, in Hammond, Indiana. Each man had been struck by a couple of .22-caliber bullets. Despite an extensive investigation, the shooter was never found

Five years later, on August 6, 1968, the killer was back, this time claiming the life of engineer John Marshall as he climbed aboard his train in Elkhart, Indiana. Several witnesses described a hulking, ape-like figure fleeing the scene, but the police were unable to find the suspect. With no clues left at the scene, the trail soon went cold.

Another three years went by before the "Railroad Sniper," reappeared. On this occasion, he drew a pistol on a railroad engineer and shot him in the arm. Despite his injuries, the engineer managed to draw his own weapon and wound his assailant.

Rudy Bladel was arrested at the scene. Tried and convicted of aggravated battery, he drew a one to five-year prison term.

Bladel served just 18 months of that sentence before being paroled in 1973. He had assumed that he'd get his old job back but was shocked and angered when he was turned down. It served only to fuel his simmering rage.

On April 5, 1976, James McCrory was sitting in the cab of his locomotive, when a shotgun blast to the back of the head ended his life. Bladel was immediately suspected but despite police surveillance, he did nothing to incriminate himself.

That would change in January 1978, when he was arrested for carrying a concealed weapon and sentenced to 11 months in prison. He served eight before being released.

By now, Bladel was convinced that the Indiana police were out to get him and he decided to move to Michigan. Within a few months of his arrival, he launched his deadliest attack yet.

On New Year's Eve, 1978, Bladel arrived at the rail yards in Jackson, Michigan, carrying a shotgun. Flagman Robert Blake and conductor William Gulak were cut down in the depot before Bladel moved to the platform. Encountering fireman Charles Burton, he opened fire immediately, killing Burton before fleeing the scene.

Given the random nature of Bladel's shooting sprees, he'd been extremely fortunate to avoid capture and again his luck held. Police in Jackson pulled him in for questioning, but Bladel answered their questions calmly and was released without charge.

Three months passed. Then in April 1979, the police finally got a break in the case when hikers found a shotgun hidden in a park outside Jackson. The weapon was traced via its serial number to Bladel, and test firing linked it to the triple homicide. Brought in for questioning, Bladel soon confessed.

Rudy Bladel went on trial in August 1979 and quickly changed his story, now claiming that he'd sold the shotgun to some unspecified individual. No one believed him. He was found guilty and sentenced to three terms of life imprisonment.

But the story had yet another twist to offer.

In 1985, the Michigan Supreme Court overturned the verdict, on the grounds that Bladel had confessed without an attorney present.

A second trial was held in June of 1987, with Bladel still sticking to his story about selling the shotgun. The second jury found that testimony no more believable than had the first. Bladel was again convicted and sentenced to three consecutive life terms. It is unlikely that he will ever be freed.

Oscar Ray Bolin

On the evening of December 4, 1986, 26-year-old Teri Lynn Matthews worked late at her job at a Tampa, Florida, bank. After work, Teri visited her boyfriend, Gary McClelland, and the couple went out to dinner before returning to the home McClelland shared with his parents.

At around 2:00 a.m., Teri left Tampa to drive to Pasco County, approximately 30 miles away, where she lived with her mother and stepfather. The drive normally took 30 to 40 minutes and she always called her boyfriend to confirm that she had arrived safely. On this particular evening, the call didn't come.

Gary McClelland waited an hour, growing more and more concerned. Eventually, he made a call to Teri, rousing her parents from sleep. A quick search of the house told them that Teri hadn't returned. McClelland then got into his car and drove towards Pasco County, following the route Teri would have taken. He eventually spotted her red Honda outside a post office in Land O'Lakes, Florida, where her parents kept a mailbox. The parking lights were on, and there was mail scattered on the ground, but there was no sign of Teri. McClelland then contacted the police.

The first clue emerged when footage from a surveillance camera showed Teri stopping at the post office on her way home. Then, as night turned to dawn came the news that the Matthews family had been dreading. The police had found a woman's body wrapped in a sheet near some railroad tracks. It was Teri Matthews.

She had been stabbed in the neck and chest, bludgeoned repeatedly over the head with a blunt instrument (later revealed to be a tire iron). An autopsy detected the presence of semen near her vaginal area, although there was no sign of rape. A DNA profile from this sample helped eliminate her boyfriend as a suspect.

The police were initially confident of making an arrest. But as days lapsed into weeks, then into months, they were no closer to catching the killer. Eventually, the trail went cold. It would remain so for five years.

In 1990, a man by the name of Danny Coby called the Florida police from Ohio. His wife, he said, had previously been married to a man named Oscar Ray Bolin, who had confessed to her that he had murdered Teri Matthews. Not only that, but Bolin's half-brother Phillip, just 13 at the time, had helped him dispose of the body.

After Phillip Bolin confirmed Coby's story, the police went looking for Oscar Ray Bolin. They found him in an Ohio prison, where he was serving a 25 to 75-year sentence for kidnapping and raping a 20-year-old waitress.

Neither was that the full extent of Bolin's crimes. As the investigation proceeded it emerged that he had killed at least two other Florida women.

Blanche Holley, 25, had been found dead in an orange grove on January 25, 1986. Seventeen-year-old Stephanie Collins disappeared from a drugstore parking lot on November 5, 1986. Her remains were found beside a rural road one month later, coincidentally on the same day that Teri Lynn Matthews' body was discovered.

Bolin was charged with all three murders and stood trial separately for each victim. In each case, he was found guilty of capital homicide and sentenced to death.

Gregg Braun

By some definitions Gregg Braun would be referred to as a spree killer rather than a serial killer, such was the ferocity of his campaign of terror. Within the space of just five blood-drenched days in 1989, Braun snuffed out the lives of five complete strangers, gunning them down for no other reason than to amuse himself.

Gregg Braun was born March 8, 1961, in Garden City, Kansas. His father, Lelyn Braun, was a prominent lawyer in that city and Gregg grew up with every advantage and privilege. After finishing high school, he attended college and obtained a law degree. There were hopes that he would follow in his father's footsteps.

But cracks were already visible in the all-American façade. The narcissistic Braun, who would later be diagnosed with borderline personality disorder, was already abusing drugs and alcohol, and was hanging with a bad crowd. Still, no one expected the carnage to follow. On July 19, 1989, whatever demons lived inside of Gregg Braun, took over.

On the day in question, Braun arrived at a convenience store in Garden City and kidnapped the clerk, 27-year-old Barbara Kochendorfer. A while later, he abducted Mary Raines, 28, from another store in the city. Each of the women was driven to a rural location and then shot in the back of the head with a .25-caliber pistol. Their bodies were dumped at the side of the road, within three miles of each other.

The following day, July 20, Braun showed up in Pampa, Texas, where he held up the one-hour photo store owned by E.P. "Pete" Spurrier. By the time he left Spurrier lay dead on the ground, killed by a bullet to the head.

Braun moved next to Oklahoma, where he robbed Dodson's Flower Shop in Ardmore. Three women were present at the time, employees Gwendolyn Sue Miller and JoAnn Beane, and customer Mary Mannings. Braun instructed them to lie face down on the floor, then shot each one in the back of the head. Beane and Mannings survived, Miller did not.

On Sunday, July 23, 1989, the roving killer was in Springer, New Mexico, where he shot and killed another convenience store clerk, 48-year-old, Geraldine Valdez. He was caught 40 minutes later, the murder weapon still in his car.

"You guys must be proud," Braun told the arresting officers. "You don't know what kind of famous criminal you caught."

Braun was questioned about the Valdez murder and soon implicated himself in the other killings. By August 3, he was the prime suspect in the murders of Kochendorfer and Rains in Kansas, Spurrier in Texas, and Miller in Oklahoma. On August 18, he was formally charged with the first-degree murder of Gwendolyn Sue Miller. Charges in the other cases followed soon after.

In the trials that ensued, Braun struck various deals to avoid the death penalty in New Mexico, Kansas, and Texas, drawing life terms instead. But he failed to do the same in Oklahoma, offering instead, a "blind plea," that is, a guilty plea without any arrangement as regards sentencing.

Perhaps, Braun believed that this guilty plea would earn him some lenience from the court. If that was the case, he was sorely mistaken.

On August 23, 1991, Judge Thomas Walker sentenced Braun to death for the murder of Gwendolyn Sue Miller. On August 27, Braun's attorneys tried to withdraw his guilty plea, but the judge denied their motion.

His subsequent appeals and requests for clemency refused, Gregg Braun was put to death by lethal injection on July 20, 2000.

Vernon Brown

Vernon Brown was born on October 1, 1953, possibly as the result of an incestuous relationship between his mother and grandfather. He grew up to be a child of low intelligence, his learning disability exacerbated by a head injury he suffered in childhood, which resulted in memory lapses.

Dropping out of school early, Brown hit the road, becoming a drifter who lived in 23 states different during the seventies. During that time he also served four years in prison for sexually assaulting a 12-year-old girl. Following that term he moved to St. Louis, Missouri where he married a homeless woman and assumed custody of her two sons.

On August 25, 1980, Brown was living in Indianapolis when 9-year-old Kimberly Campbell was found raped and strangled in a vacant house owned by Brown's grandmother. Brown had been

seen with the child the previous day but in the absence of solid
evidence the police had to let the case drop.

A year later, warrants were issued against Brown for six counts of
child molestation and he promptly skipped town, returning to St.
Louis. There, he assumed the alias Thomas Turner, and found
work as a janitor at an apartment building on Washington Avenue.

On March 7, 1985, 19-year-old Synetta Ford was found dead in her
basement apartment. She'd been strangled to death with an
electrical cord and stabbed several times in the chest and throat.
With little evidence left at the scene, investigators had low
expectations of solving the crime. That is until Vernon Brown's
wife phoned the police and claimed that he had admitted the
murder to her.

Brown was brought in for questioning but steadfastly maintained
his innocence. As Missouri law prohibits spousal testimony and as
there was no evidence to corroborate the charges, the police were
forced to let him go. Unfortunately, that decision would have tragic
consequences.

At around 3 p.m. on October 24, 1986, Brown collected his
stepsons from the Cole School in north St. Louis. While doing so, he
spotted 9-year-old Janet Perkins, who lived less than a block from
the Brown residence and usually passed their house on her way
home from school.

Brown rushed home, sent his sons inside and waited until Janet
passed by just a few minutes later. He then coaxed her into the

house, possibly on the pretense of speaking to his sons, who were known to her.

Once he had the little girl inside, Brown sent his boys to their room and locked them in. He then took Janet down to the basement, where he bound her hands and feet with a coat hanger. He then raped her, before strangling her to death with a length of rope. Her body was found the following day, discarded in a dumpster.

How Brown thought he would get away with the crime is difficult to gauge. A neighbor had seen him lure the little girl into his house and his sons had heard her screams as he'd brutalized her. Arrested soon after the discovery of the body, he fell back on the oldest excuse of all. He claimed that he had blacked out under the influence of drugs (PCP, in this case).

That defense carried little weight with the jury. They found him guilty of capital murder and the judge passed sentence of death. He was subsequently tried for the murder of Synetta Ford, drawing another death sentence.

Brown was executed by lethal injection in Missouri on May 17, 2005. Following his death, Indianapolis police closed their file on the Kimberly Campbell murder. He is also suspected in the murder of 15-year-old Tracey Poindexter, killed in Indianapolis during April 1985, and in another homicide from August of that year.

Robert Browne

Robert Browne was not a man who believed in doing things by half measure. One of nine children (including three sets of twins) the Coushatta, Louisiana, native had been married six times. Now he was claiming to have killed 49 people over a 25-year span.

The reason that Browne's murder spree had not attracted attention earlier was two-fold. Firstly, he kept on the move, committing murders in nine different states as well as in Korea. Second, he varied his method, killing by "every method known to man," according to one investigator. And he might well have gotten away with it, had he not decided to draw attention to himself.

Already serving a life term in Colorado for the 1991 murder of 13-year-old Heather Dawn Church, Browne sent a letter to the authorities in 2000. "Seven sacred virgins entombed side by side, those less worthy are scattered wide," he wrote, enclosing a hand drawn map with outlines of Colorado, Washington, California, New Mexico, Texas, Oklahoma, Louisiana, Arkansas, and Mississippi, with his body count written inside each state, totaling 49 victims.

At first, investigators were skeptical. Prisoners are always talking themselves up, claiming crimes they didn't commit. The Henry Lee Lucas and Donald Evans debacles were still fresh in many people's minds.

But once they sat down with Browne, it was clear that he knew things about many of the crimes that only the killer would know. And as investigators looked deeper into the cases he claimed to be responsible for, they realized that many could be definitively linked to Browne.

Some of those were:

Katherine Hayes, 15: Reported missing on July 4, 1980, her body was found in Nantachie Creek on October 16, 1980. She had been strangled.

Wanda Faye Hudson, 21: Found dead in her Coushatta, Louisiana apartment on May 28, 1983. Coushatta is Browne's hometown and he had worked as a maintenance man in Hudson's apartment building, even changing the lock on her door.

Faye Self, 26: Reported missing in Louisiana on March 30, 1983. Browne told the authorities that he dumped her body in the Red River. She has never been found.

Melody Bush, 22: Found dead in a drainage ditch in Fayette County, Texas, on March 30, 1984. The coroner ruled that she had died of acetone poisoning.

Nidia Mendoza, 17: Reported missing on February 2, 1984, in Texas. Her body was discovered in a ditch four days later.

Lisa Lowe, 21: Reported missing in Arkansas on November 3, 1991. Her body was found November 26, 1991, in the St. Francis River.

Rocio Sperry, 15: Went missing from El Paso County, Texas, on November 15, 1987. Browne said he strangled her in his apartment before dumping her body in a trash bin. She has never been found.

Browne was eventually tried and convicted of the Sperry murder, adding an additional life term to his sentence. In the other cases, investigators declined to press charges, due to lack of evidence. Browne's recollections of these crimes were too vague for the police to follow up on.

However, if Browne's confession to 49 murders is to be believed, it would place him among the most prolific serial killers in American history.

Gary Ridgeway, the infamous Green River Killer confessed to 48 murders but privately admitted to 71. Randy Kraft, California's notorious "Scorecard Killer," kept detailed records of the 66 murders he committed. Other notorious killers, like Ted Bundy, are suspected of many more murders than those they were tried for.

Robert F. Carr

"In my 33-year career in law enforcement, he ranks as the most dangerous child sexual predator I ever investigated."

Those were the words of David Simmons, the veteran homicide detective who arrested Robert Carr. And yet Carr came across as anything but dangerous. The slightly built television repairman with the wispy red hair, was soft-spoken and charming, all the better to lure his young victims.

In common with many serial killers, Carr showed signs of aberrant behavior early in life, taking out his murderous impulses on animals. By the age of 11, he was prostituting himself to pedophiles; by his teens, he was stealing cars.

It seemed inevitable that this downward spiral would lead to more serious crimes, and so it proved. Between 1973 and 1975, he was imprisoned for a rape in Connecticut. Paroled from that prison term, he moved to Miami.

Carr was married by now, but the sex he had with his wife did nothing to alleviate his fantasies about abducting and raping young boys. He began cruising Biscayne Boulevard, the passenger door of his car rigged so that it couldn't be opened from the inside.

On November 13, 1972, he was trolling the strip when he encountered 11-year- olds Todd Payton and Mark Wilson hitchhiking. Carr stopped to give them a ride and then either persuaded or coerced them into joining him on an extended road trip. Over the next 10 days, he raped, tortured and eventually murdered the boys.

Todd was the first to die, strangled and confined to a shallow grave in Mississippi. Four days later, Mark suffered the same fate, his body buried in Louisiana. It is difficult to imagine the terror the boy must have felt during those four days, knowing that it was only a matter of time before his abductor killed him.

Carr was eventually arrested in 1976, when a Metro police officer caught him in the act of raping a Miami housewife. In custody, he quickly confessed to murdering Todd and Mark and added two more victims, 16-year-old Tammy Ruth Huntley, and 21-year-old Rhonda Holloway. He also admitted to raping over a dozen young boys and girls.

As part of a plea deal that would save him from the electric chair, Carr later led officers on a cross-country sojourn to the burial sites of his victims; Todd Payton in Mississippi, Mark Wilson in Louisiana, Tammy Ruth Huntley buried in a shallow grave, also in Mississippi. Rhonda Holloway was found in Connecticut, fully clothed, her hands and feet still bound. She had been Carr's first victim.

Although Carr avoided the death penalty by cooperating with the authorities, the sentence handed down by the court was one of the most severe in Florida history. He was given a prison term amounting to 1,400 years, meaning he'd (theoretically) be ineligible for parole until July 30, 3414.

Carr served his sentence at Union Correctional Institution in North Florida. His time in prison was not easy. Reviled as a child murderer, he was initially held in the prison hospital but was removed from there after authorities uncovered an escape plot.

He died in prison on July 6, 2007, at the age of 63. Unsurprisingly, no one claimed his body and he was buried in the prison cemetery.

Vernon Clark

Elkridge, Maryland, is a quaint little town of antique shops and elegant 19th-century houses, which lies five miles southwest of Baltimore. It is hardly the kind of setting where you'd expect to find a series of brutal murders. And yet, over a ten-year period, from April 1979 to July 1989, just such a spree occurred here.

The killer first announced his deadly presence with a double homicide, killing Carvel Faulkner and his wife, Sarah, on April 26, 1979. Carvel, aged 58, was found on the floor of his bedroom, a bullet wound to his head. His wife was lying in a pool of blood on the bed. Her hands and feet were bound and her throat had been slit. There was no sign of forced entry and $1,000 in cash, lying in plain view, was untouched.

Less than a year later, on February 15, 1980, another elderly Elkridge resident was slain. The victim was Rebecca "Dolly" Davis, a 72-year-old portrait painter, who lived in the affluent Lawyer's Hill area. She'd been sexually assaulted and stabbed to death. Her body was found partially buried near her house.

Another year passed before the killer struck again. Evelyn Dietrich lived just a few miles from Dolly Davis. Her body was found concealed in bushes in her garden. She'd been bludgeoned and strangled.

By now, the police were certain that a single perpetrator was responsible. Thirty officers were assigned to the case, traveling as far afield as Texas in pursuit of leads. Officers staked out Davis' gravesite on the anniversary of her death, hoping the killer might show up. They even brought in a psychic. They came up empty.

Eventually, the investigation ground to a halt. The evidence was boxed and consigned to storage in the police department's property room. The murders, too, appeared to have wound down. It seemed the killer would never be caught.

Nearly four years later, on December 28, 1984, the partially clothed body of 80-year-old Iva Myrtle Watson was found in a pine grove a block from her home in nearby Ellicott City. Iva had lived just a block away from the Faulkners. She'd been sexually assaulted and beaten to death.

Another four and a half years passed before a seemingly unrelated murder occurred. Kathleen Gouldin was just 23 years old on the night of July 4, 1989, when an intruder broke into her Elkridge apartment and assaulted her before shooting her to death.

The killer was quickly apprehended, nabbed by fingerprints left on a pizza box.

He was Vernon Lee Clark, a 43-year-old who worked as a sometime handyman. Clark was convicted of the murder and sentenced to life imprisonment.

In 2001, cold case investigators sent semen collected from the Dolly Davis murder scene for DNA analysis. Not long after, they had a match. The semen was from convicted felon, Vernon Lee Clark, currently serving life for the murder of Kathleen Gouldin.

Confronted with the evidence, Clark struck a deal to avoid the death penalty, accepting an additional life term instead. DNA evidence subsequently linked him to Evelyn Dietrich's murder. It also emerged that he had known each of his victims. He had done handyman work for Davis, Dietrich, and Watson, and had lived near the Faulkners.

Clark is currently serving his time at the Maryland Department of Corrections Annex in Jessup. He will never be released.

Alfred Cline

The idea may seem quaint now, but from the mid-1800's to the middle of the 20th century, any number of "Bluebeard" serial killers plied their deadly trade around the globe. France had Landru, England had George Joseph Smith and America had Harry Powers and Johan Hoch, among others. Another who fits this mold is Alfred Cline, the so-called "Buttermilk Bluebeard."

Born in 1888, Cline was active between 1930 and 1945, claiming at least nine victims across California, Nevada, Texas, Massachusetts, and Colorado. His modus operandi was the typical woo them, wed them, fleece them, kill them, of this type of serial killer. Where Cline differed was that he was exceedingly careful. Despite all the evidence against him, he was never tried for murder.

What exactly attracted so many lonely women to the middle-aged, heavy-set Cline is unknown, but he was said to wield a certain romantic charm, which his favorite type of victim – lonely, well-heeled older women – found irresistible. He'd court them at church functions and socials, declare his undying love and quickly propose. Any woman who accepted was effectively signing her own death warrant.

Cline would whisk her off for an extravagant honeymoon, book into a top-notch hotel and then put his plan into action. His M.O. seldom varied. First, he'd insist that his bride drink a glass of buttermilk, which he had earlier laced with a powerful tranquilizer. Then, once the unfortunate woman lost consciousness, he'd summon the house physician, claim that his wife suffered from a heart complaint, and insist that she'd had a heart attack.

Hours later, he'd deliver a second more powerful dose of sedatives. The doctor would again be called and arrive to find the patient dead. Eager to avoid a scandal for the hotel, most would quickly issue a death certificate citing 'heart failure' as the cause of death. Thereafter, Cline would hastily arrange a cremation, so that there could be no possibility of an autopsy.

Cline successfully ran this scam at least seven times between 1930 and 1944, each time netting himself a tidy inheritance. He also claimed his only male victim during this time, an evangelist minister who had bequeathed $11,000 to him in his will.

In May 1944, Cline married a Chicago widow by the name of
Delora Krebs. Soon after the wedding, he set off for San Francisco
with his new bride, who presumably met the same fate as her
predecessors.

But in this case, Cline had miscalculated. Delora's family became
concerned when they couldn't reach her on the phone and began
pestering Cline as to her whereabouts. For a time, he fobbed them
off by telling them that Delora was ill, or out shopping, or
otherwise engaged. Eventually, as their calls became more and
more insistent, Cline informed them that Delora had died of
natural causes.

Dissatisfied with this explanation (especially as Delora's annuity
checks were still being cashed) her relatives went to the
authorities. The subsequent investigation would uncover the trail
of death that Cline had left across the country.

However, despite overwhelming evidence of wrongdoing, the
absence of a body meant that Cline could not be successfully tried
for murder. He could, however, be tried for forgery, as he'd
continued to cash Delora's checks after her death.

In a classic case of poetic justice, Cline's greed came back to haunt
him when he received the maximum term of 126 years. He died of
a heart attack at Folsom Prison on August 5, 1948.

Jerome Dennis

Although some serial killers range far and wide in their hunt for victims, most prefer areas that they are familiar with. In this regard, they are similar to predators of the animal world, staking out a territory and stalking it for prey. One such a creature was working an isolated corridor in East Orange, New Jersey, in late 1991 and early 1992.

Over a period of just five months, the killer struck repeatedly, leaving five women dead, and others injured and traumatized. The bodies were found in desolate, poorly lit areas under rail trestles or along highway embankments, all of them within walking distance of the East Orange police station. When an arrest was eventually made, investigators would realize another significant detail about the killer's chosen hunting ground. All but one of the victims were found within a few blocks of the killer's home.

The first attack occurred on December 12, 1991. The 26-year-old victim was raped and beaten but survived. Just two days later, another woman was not so lucky. Robyn Carter, 41, was found in Newark on December 16. She'd been raped, beaten, and stabbed to death.

Following the murder of Robyn Carter, the killer went to ground, perhaps contemplating his crime, perhaps fearful of being caught. He emerged again on February 22, although on this occasion the 23-year-old rape victim escaped with her life. She described her attacker as a short, slim, black man.

Over the next six weeks, while police hunted for the rapist, three more women disappeared from the streets of East Orange. Then, in the early hours of Friday, April 10, a patrolman found the body of 16-year-old high school student, Jamillah Jones, on an East Orange street. She'd been stabbed to death.

As police widened their search for clues, they discovered another corpse. She was identified as 30-year-old Elizabeth Clenor, reported missing by her mother on February 17. She'd been killed by a blow to the head.

Later that same afternoon, a third body, that of Stephanie Alston, 30, was found. And the following day brought yet another gruesome discovery, a badly decomposed corpse concealed among the weeds near Oraton Parkway.

With police now certain that they had a serial killer in their midst, a task force was rapidly established and almost immediately produced results.

On Sunday, April 12, police arrested Jerome Dennis, an ex-con currently on parole for a 1981 rape. Dennis was put into a police lineup and picked out right away by two of his surviving victims. Faced with the evidence, he confessed and was charged with multiple counts of murder.

Jerome Dennis had been in trouble with the law since his early teens. The seventh-grade dropout was one of nine children and had grown up in one of the poorest neighborhoods in Newark.

In November 1981, Dennis and one of his brothers had been arrested for a series of brutal rapes. Dennis, just 14 at the time, was sentenced to 30 years in prison, serving the mandatory minimum of ten years before his release on November 19, 1991.

Dennis had been a model prisoner at the Yardville State Prison but had immediately reverted to type once he was free. He'd carried out his first attack within weeks of his release.

Dennis would eventually be convicted of five counts of first-degree murder. On March 2, 1993, he was sentenced to life in prison without the possibility of parole.

Paul Durousseau

When 19-year-old Nikia Kilpatrick didn't show up for a get-
together on New Year's Day 2003, her family was worried and
went looking for her. Arriving at Nikia's Jacksonville apartment
their concern was elevated when they saw Nikia's two-year-old
son desperately banging on the inside of the glass sliding door. As
they forced the door open, they immediately became aware of an
overpoweringly rancid smell.

A search of the home soon revealed its source. Nikia's body lay on
the floor, her hands tied and a cord knotted tightly around her
neck. Her other son, just 11 months old, crawled on the floor
nearby.

An autopsy would later reveal that Nikia, 6 months pregnant at the
time of her death, had been raped. Her young children, although

unharmed, were suffering from dehydration and malnutrition and were quite obviously traumatized by their ordeal.

The brutal and organized nature of the crime concerned homicide investigators who believed that the perpetrator had killed before and would likely do so again. They were proven right in that assumption just ten days later.

On January 10, 2003, 23-year-old nursing assistant, Shawanda McCalister, was found strangled to death in her apartment. The crime was startlingly similar to the Kilpatrick murder, right down to the distinctive knots in the ligature. It was almost certain that the same man was responsible.

With this in mind, investigators began looking into other unsolved homicides and soon picked up one that was probably linked. Eighteen-year-old Nicole Williams had been found on December 19, 2002, her body wrapped in a blanket. The knots used to tie her hands were the same as those in the other two cases, and DNA evidence soon backed up the single perpetrator theory. Jacksonville had a serial killer on its streets.

Victim number four turned up on February 5, 2003. She was 17-year-old Jovanna Jefferson, her body discovered at a construction site on New Kings Road.

But Jovanna's was not the only body found at the site. Just six feet away lay the decomposing remains of another woman (later identified as 19-year-old Surita Ann Cohen). Crime scene evidence linked these two victims to the others, bringing the Jacksonville serial killer's deadly toll to five.

Shortly after these last two murders the police finally had a suspect. A witness came forward to say that he'd seen both Jovanna and Surita in the company of a cab driver named Paul Durousseau.

Looking into Durousseau's background, detectives learned that he was married with two children and had served in the Army. They also discovered that he had a long rap sheet, including arrests for assault, kidnapping, and rape. Even more interesting was that Durousseau had been a murder suspect while serving at Fort Benning, Georgia. There had been insufficient evidence to charge him, but not long after, he'd been found in possession of stolen goods and dishonorably discharged.

Durousseau had struggled to find employment after being thrown out of the military. Eventually, he had moved his family to Jacksonville, where he'd gotten a job as a school bus driver. There were problems in his marriage, though. In August 1999 and again in March 2001, Durousseau was arrested for assaulting his wife.

Durousseau looked like a promising suspect. And the case against him was firmed up even more, when it transpired that Jovanna Jefferson had been picked up by a taxi driver on the night of her disappearance, someone she referred to only as "D."

"D" as it turned out, was a nickname commonly used by Paul Durousseau.

The police weren't yet ready to charge Durousseau with murder but they wanted him off the streets before he had the chance to kill again. The excuse to arrest him came when he violated his parole for a 2001 rape case.

With Durousseau in custody, the full weight of forensic, physical, and DNA evidence was brought to bear and he was charged with five counts of first-degree murder. Two counts were later added to the indictment, after DNA linked him to murders committed in Georgia and Florida.

Durousseau was tried and found guilty on all counts. He was sentenced to die by lethal injection and currently awaits execution at Florida's Union Correctional Institution.

50 American Monsters You've Probably Never Heard Of Volume 5

Nancy Farrer

Nancy Farrer had been burdened with incredibly bad genes in the looks department, her appearance described as grotesque, with a misshapen head and large bulging eyes. Yet despite these impediments, she'd gained a reputation as an able and reliable nurse, even considering the fact that people had a habit of dying in the households where she served.

In 1851, Nancy entered the service of Elisha Forrest and his family. Nancy had previously been described as an affectionate sort who never back-chatted her employers and seldom spoke unless spoken to. Yet, within a week at her new job, Mrs. Forrest had managed to annoy her in some way, leading Nancy to confide in a friend that she would "fix her."

Shortly after that exchange, Mrs. Forrest fell ill after eating a meal that Nancy had prepared. As the poor woman took to her bed, complaining of stomach pains, and was given to bouts of projectile vomiting, Nancy was heard to remark that it was "just like Mrs. Green." Mrs. Green, Nancy's previous employer, had died recently in mysterious circumstances. The following day, Mrs. Forrest was also dead.

A week after Mrs. Forrest's funeral, her son, John Edward Forrest, was ill with startlingly similar symptoms. He died in great pain shortly after. Nancy, though professing to be saddened by his death, predicted more tragedy for the Forrest household. "Jimmy will go next, then Billy, then the old man," she foretold.

A short while later, Jimmy Forrest, hale and hearty up to that point, developed symptoms similar to his mother and brother. At the same time, Elisha and Billy Forrest both became violently ill, after eating a meal that Nancy had prepared but refused to partake of.

When Jimmy died in agony after consuming an elixir of "onion syrup" that Nancy had given him, Elisha had had enough. He demanded an autopsy on his son and that autopsy showed that Jimmy had died of arsenic poisoning.

Almost immediately, suspicion fell on Nancy. Then, after a druggist's wrapper was discovered in her room, it was determined that she had purchased five cents worth of arsenic from a drugstore, ostensibly for killing rats. Other druggists soon testified to purchases from their establishments, some going back as far as six months. All in all, Nancy had bought enough poison to kill

twenty people. In short order, she found herself on trial for
murder.

Nancy Farrar's trial caused a major stir in the city of Cincinnati,
then a community of some 120,000. There was very little question
as to her guilt. The main issue regarded her sanity and, in the
custom of the day, that was for the jury to determine.

They eventually decided that Farrar was sane and therefore
responsible for her actions. The likelihood was that she would
hang.

Fortunately for Farrar, the judge held a different opinion. After
berating the jury for several instances of misconduct (which
included intoxication, reading newspaper accounts of the case
while deliberating, and colluding with the prosecution), he
dismissed their ruling and declared Farrar "not guilty by reason of
insanity."

History does not record what happened to Nancy. Given the
protocols in place at the time, it is likely that she saw out her days
as an inmate in an insane asylum.

Lorenzo Fayne

"The things I done, I deserve to die, really I do." Those were the words of Lorenzo Fayne, serial killer and necrophile, as he stood trial for the brutal murders of five children.

Fayne was born in Milwaukee, Wisconsin, in 1970. As a child, he suffered horrendous physical abuse at the hands of both of his parents. His mother and stepfather were alcoholics and his mother was also addicted to crack cocaine. Even before he reached his teens Fayne was using both substances himself.

At 7, Fayne was raped by a neighborhood boy four years his senior. From the age of 13, he was in and out of legal custody, charged with such offenses as shoplifting, assault, indecent exposure, housebreaking, and car theft. Like many fledgling serial killers, he was also fond of abusing animals.

When Fayne was 18, he began drifting between Milwaukee and East St. Louis, Illinois, where his grandmother lived. That was in 1989, the year he also committed his first murder.

The victim was Aree Hunt, a six-year-old boy lured from a playground and then sexually assaulted and bludgeoned to death, his body thrown into a ditch. When Fayne eventually confessed to the crime, he said he'd killed the boy because he wanted to hear the sound of a neck snapping.

Over the next three years, Fayne would claim five more victims, four of them children.

Latondra Dean's body was discovered in a bathtub in March 1992. The 14-year-old had been raped and then stabbed more than twenty times in the chest.

Nine-year-old Fallon Flood was found inside an abandoned locker room at East St. Louis Senior High School in July 1992. She had been strangled with a belt and her underwear was around her ankles. Fayne would later admit to trying to rape her.

The severely decomposed body of Glenda Jones, 17, was found behind Martin Luther King Junior High near the boundary between East St. Louis and Centreville in June 1993. She had been stabbed to death. Fayne later confessed to having sex with her corpse.

The murder that would eventually lead to Fayne's arrest occurred in July 1994, just a block away from where he'd killed Latondra

Dean. Seventeen-year-old Faith Davis was stabbed to death in the bathtub at her friend's home. Fayne then raped and sodomized the corpse before fleeing the scene, but returned a short while later, to have sex with the dead body again. On this occasion, he set the house on fire before leaving, a bad move, as it turned out.

Firefighters were called to the scene and soon discovered Davis's body. Then the police arrived and used a police dog to follow a trail of blood from the burning house. It led directly to the home of Lorenzo Fayne's grandmother.

Fayne was tried separately for each murder. In the Aree Hunt case, he received a life sentence when one of the jurors refused to vote for the death penalty. In each of the other cases, he was sentenced to death.

Lorenzo Fayne has since been linked by DNA evidence to another murder, that of 32-year-old mother of three, Rita Scott. Scott's partially clothed body was found lying in a pool of blood on September 15, 1989. Her head had been caved in with a chunk of concrete, and she had been sexually assaulted post-mortem. Confronted with the evidence, Fayne readily confessed.

Lorenzo Gilyard

It is a sad indictment of the times we live in, when a serial killer as prolific as Lorenzo Gilyard goes almost unnoticed. Over a 16-year period, from 1977 to 1993, Gilyard terrorized Kansas City, Missouri, strangling to death at least 13 women, all but one of them prostitutes.

The first victim was 17-year-old Stacie Swofford, killed in April 1977, her body dumped in a garbage-strewn lot. Three years later, Gwen Kizine, a 15-year-old just starting out in the dangerous world of prostitution, was found dead in an alleyway. Another teenaged prostitute, Margaret Miller, died at the hands of the same killer in May 1982.

Whether or not the police identified the three murders as a series, is unknown. Before any headway was made in the investigation, the killings suddenly stopped.

They resumed four years later, on March 14, 1986. The fourth victim, 34-year-old, Catherine Barry was not a prostitute, but she was homeless and living on the streets, easy prey for a serial killer.

In August 1986, another prostitute, 23-year-old Naomi Kelly showed up dead, her body discarded in a downtown park popular with drug addicts. Fourteen weeks later, the naked corpse of Debbie Blevins, 32, turned up outside a church in fashionable Westport.

The new year brought no respite from the killings. Five women – Ann Barnes, 36,

Kellie Ann Ford, 20, Angela Mayhew, 19, Sheila Ingold, 36, and Carmeline Hibbs, 30, were found murdered in 1987. All were prostitutes. All had been strangled.

By now, the police knew that they were dealing with a serial killer, but their response to the situation was tepid at best. Neither was the media particularly interested in the murder spree happening in their city. The Kansas City Strangler did attract some attention in the press but, as is often the case with prostitute victims, the coverage was muted. It was hardly the outcry you'd expect after ten brutal murders.

Over a year passed before the killer struck again. The victim was another prostitute, 26-year-old Austrian national, Helga Kruger. And four more years would pass before the last victim, Connie Luther, was found dead in January 1993. Thereafter, the killings stopped entirely.

By 2003, the Kansas City Strangler investigation had long been consigned to a cold case file, with little prospect of a resolution. DNA technology had, of course, advanced to the point where cold cases were being revisited and solved all over the country, but the Kansas City Police Department simply lacked the funds to reopen its hundreds of cold cases.

All of that changed in 2003, when the department was given $111,000 in federal funding, enabling it to run DNA tests on evidence from unsolved homicides. One of the cases chosen for evaluation was the 1986 murder of Naomi Kelly.

A match was soon obtained to a man named Lorenzo Gilyard, an ex-con who had served four years for felony assault. But then lab technicians got an unexpected bonus, linking Gilyard to twelve other murders, including all of the Kansas City Strangler killings.

Gilyard was well known to the Kansas City Police Department. He had, in fact, been a suspect at the height of the prostitute murders. Aside from that, he'd racked up a long list of rape arrests and yet had always managed to avoid serious jail time until his assault conviction in 1982. The four years he'd been away had coincidentally matched the break in the prostitute murders.

Gilyard was arrested in 2004. Aware that he'd likely face the death penalty if found guilty, his lawyers asked for a deal. Gilyard would waive his right to a jury trial, as well as his right of appeal, if the prosecutor did not seek the death penalty.

Jackson County Prosecutor Jim Kanatzar agreed, but it would be a full three years before the matter eventually came to trial in 2007. Charged with seven murders, Gilyard was found guilty of six. He was sentenced to life in prison without the possibility of parole.

Josephine Gray

Although Josephine Gray was never charged with murder, there can be little doubt that she was complicit in the deaths of three men, deaths that benefitted her to the tune of $165,000. Yet, for over 26 years, no one was prepared to testify against Gray, afraid as they were of her reputed use of voodoo to exact revenge against those who crossed her.

The first victim of this classic 'Black Widow' was her husband, Norman Stribbling. In the weeks prior to his death, Stribbling had confided in friends that Josephine had tried to shoot him and that he'd only survived because the gun had misfired.

Then, on March 3, 1974, he was dead, killed by a single gunshot wound to the head. Gray was immediately a suspect, especially when it emerged that she'd tried to hire a contract killer to get rid of her husband. But despite strong circumstantial evidence, the DA decided that a murder case against Gray would not be winnable.

Gray was not only a free woman but also $16,000 richer, courtesy of Stribbling's life insurance policy.

In November 1975, Josephine remarried. Husband number two was William Gray, a man with whom she'd been having an affair while married to Norman Stribbling. The couple would remain together for fifteen years. By the time they separated, in August 1990, there were familiar echoes, harking back to Josephine's previous marriage. Josephine was having an affair (this time with a co-worker, Clarence Goode), her husband was heavily insured, and he was complaining to friends that Josephine was trying to kill him.

In October 1990, a few weeks before his murder, William Gray filed a complaint with Montgomery County police. In it, he claimed that his estranged wife had attacked him with a screwdriver and a baseball bat. He also said that she and her boyfriend had chased him in her car and that the boyfriend (Goode) had pointed a gun at him.

While the police investigated these allegations, William Gray got to work removing his wife as the beneficiary of his insurance policies. He wasn't quick enough.

On November 9, 1990, he was found shot to death in his apartment. Despite being a suspect in his murder, Josephine Gray collected over $54,000 in life insurance.

Following a now familiar pattern, Josephine moved in with Clarence Goode and although they never married, the couple remained together until 1996. In March, of that year, Goode applied for a $100,000 life insurance policy, naming Josephine Gray as the sole beneficiary. On June 21, 1996, he was found dead in the trunk of his car in Baltimore. He had been shot in the head.

Gray received $90,000 from her former lover's insurance policy, the remaining $10,000 going to Goode's minor son.

It soon emerged that the death of Clarence Goode had once again followed Josephine Gray's well-trodden path to murder. Prior to Goode's death, Gray had become involved with a new lover, Andre Savoy. She'd also begun threatening Goode, at one stage menacing him with a knife. Clarence Goode had moved out, and stopped payment on his insurance premiums. Before the policy lapsed, he'd been killed, ensuring that Josephine got her payout.

Several weeks after Goode's death, a search warrant was executed at Josephine Gray's residence. Investigators found a large stain on the concrete floor of the garage, which tested positive for blood. They also found blood inside a vacuum cleaner. However, this evidence was deemed insufficient to bring charges. It appeared that Josephine had gotten away with murder yet again.

But Federal investigators were not about to let her get off that easily. They charged her with federal mail and wire fraud violations, relating to collecting money on the deaths of the three men. This meant that the jury did not have to decide whether Gray had committed murder. All that had to decide was whether she had played a role in the men's deaths and was therefore disallowed from collecting insurance benefits under the so-called 'Slayer's Rule.'

Faced with this lesser burden of truth, the jury found Josephine Gray guilty. She was sentenced to 40 years in prison.

Ricky Lee Green

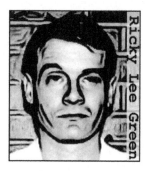

Childhood abuse is often cited as a contributing factor in the making of a serial killer and in the case of Ricky Lee Green, it certainly seems to have played a part. Green suffered horrible abuse – verbal, physical and sexual – at the hands of his father and grandfather. An example of this was a game his father liked to play. He'd instruct the 6-year-old to run and hide. Then he'd stalk the boy and shoot him with a BB gun. Later, when Ricky was sent to live with his grandfather, the older man kept up the abuse, regularly sodomizing his grandson.

Despite these childhood travails, Ricky Lee hoped for a stable life with a wife and family. On February 18, 1984, he married Mary Francis, a union that lasted only two months before she walked out, accusing him of spousal rape. Two weeks after Mary's departure he hooked up with Sharon Dollar, a woman who shared his appetite for sadomasochistic sex.

Green committed his first known murder in April 1985. The victim was a 16-year-old by the name of Jeffrey Davis. According to Green, he invited the teen to hang out with him while Sharon was out of town. The two went cruising in Green's car. However, after Green stopped to urinate beside the road, he returned to find Davis masturbating in the passenger seat. Davis then asked if Green wanted to touch him, causing Green to lose his temper and beat him.

They drove for a while, eventually stopping at a secluded spot where Green decided to kill the youth. Pulling Davis from the car, he beat and stabbed him, then cut off his penis and threw it into a lake. He disposed of the body nearby.

In September 1985, Green and Sharon Dollar married. A month later, Green was driving near Fort Worth when he picked up a 28-year-old topless dancer named Betty Jo Monroe. He invited her home where he had sex with her. When Sharon arrived she was surprised to find another woman in the house. However, she agreed to Green's suggestion of a threesome.

Monroe was initially agreeable too, but then changed her mind. This angered Green and he attacked her with a knife and then struck her with a hammer. Sharon, according to Green, was a full participant in the murder. Later, the two of them had sex beside the corpse.

The next victim was 27-year-old Sandra Bailey, who Green picked up at a country and western bar in November 1985. Sandra agreed to go home with him for sex, but shirked when she saw Sharon and realized that Green wanted a threesome. She was killed in much the same manner as Betty Jo Monroe, with Sharon again a full participant. The couple again had sex beside to the woman's mutilated corpse.

On December 27, 1986, Green picked up Steven Fefferman, an advertising executive, at a Casino Beach parking lot frequented by homosexuals.

Green agreed to go back to Fefferman's house. Once there he asked Fefferman if he would mind being tied up during sex. Fefferman agreed, but as soon as he was bound, Green produced a knife and started telling him how much he hated homosexuals. He began stabbing and mutilating Fefferman with the knife, slitting him open from sternum to scrotum. He then cut off Fefferman's penis and shoved it into the man's mouth while he was still alive. After ransacking the apartment, he fled.

Returning home, Green told Sharon about the murder. He'd soon have cause to regret his boasts. Their relationship went swiftly downhill after that and after Sharon walked out, she contacted the police, struck a deal and confessed her part in the crimes. In short order, Ricky Lee found himself under arrest and charged with murder.

He'd eventually receive three life terms, one for each of the Davis, Monroe, and Bailey homicides. For the Fefferman murder, he was sentenced to die by lethal injection. For her part in the brutal slayings, Sharon got 10 years probation.

Ricky Lee Green was put to death by lethal injection on October 8, 1997. He remains the prime suspect in eight other murders committed in the area.

Randy Greenawalt

Randy Greenawalt was already a convicted serial killer by the time he launched the deadly killing spree that would catapult him towards infamy. Serving a life term for the 1974 slaying of a trucker, Greenawalt admitted to two more murders, one in Arizona, the other in Colorado.

Once inside, the highly intelligent Greenawalt befriended Gary Gene Tison, a feared and respected inmate serving life for the murder of a police officer. The two began talking about escape, lamenting the fact that as lifers, they were never likely to get the opportunity.

Then, in 1978, Greenawalt and Tison's luck took a turn for the better when they were transferred to a low-security Trusty Unit. They immediately began plotting their escape, roping in Tison's sons Donny, Ricky, and Ray to help.

On July 30, the Tison boys visited their father in prison. Donald, 20, carried an icebox, ostensibly holding a picnic lunch. While checking in for the visit, he suddenly threw the box open and withdrew a sawn-off shotgun. While Donald and Raymond assisted their father in binding and gagging the guards, Greenawalt disabled the telephones and alarm system. Then the five of them walked so casually out of the prison that perimeter guards thought they were departing visitors.

Their plan was to obtain a plane and fly to Mexico. When this fell through, they decided to drive across the border. Unfortunately for them, and for the six people they'd encounter, their vehicle suffered a flat tire before they reached California.

Marine Sergeant John F. Lyons, 24, was driving to his home in Yuma, Arizona, when he encountered the fugitives stranded at the side of the road. Lyons made the fateful decision to stop and offer assistance. Immediately, he was overpowered.

Greenawalt and Tison then proceeded to execute Lyons, his wife Donnelda, 24, and the couple's 22-month-old son Christopher. All were shot in the back of the head with a shotgun. Lyons' 15-year-old niece, Teresa Tyson, suffered a gunshot wound to her hip as she tried to escape. Mortally wounded and in extreme pain, she dragged herself a quarter mile into the desert before succumbing to her injuries.

With one of the biggest manhunts in Arizona history now underway, the escapees drove to Colorado where they robbed and murdered a honeymooning couple, James Judge Jr. and his wife Margene. They then headed back to Arizona.

The police meanwhile had set up a roadblock near Tison's hometown of Casa Grande, Arizona. On August 11, 1978, a silver van approached the roadblock, slowing when the police signaled them to do so. Then, as the van got closer, the driver suddenly put his foot down and they burst through.

The officers immediately radioed their colleagues, positioned five miles down the road. This time, the police opened fire, killing the driver, Donny Tison. A half hour gun battle ensued until eventually Greenawalt, along with Ricky and Ray Tison, surrendered.

Gary Tison, meanwhile, had fled into the desert. His bloated corpse was found two days later. He was uninjured and had apparently died of exposure and dehydration.

Greenawalt and the surviving Tison sons, Raymond and Ricky, were tried, found guilty and sentenced to death. The Tisons' death sentences were subsequently commuted to life in prison.

For Randy Greenwaldt though, there would be no escape. He spent 19 years running through various appeals in a vain attempt to have his sentence overturned. He was executed by lethal injection on January 23, 1997.

Richard Grissom

When Richard Grissom was just 16 years old, he murdered an elderly woman in Lansing, Kansas. Hazel Meeker was a neighbor of the Grissom family. She was found stabbed and beaten to death with a railroad spike. Arrested for the crime, Grissom spent just two years in a juvenile prison. In 1968, aged 18, he walked free, his record permanently sealed. It was as though the murder never happened.

Over the next decade, Grissom was in and out of trouble with the law, mainly for petty thefts and burglaries. By 1989 he was a handsome, but arrogant, young man who ran a small maintenance business and enjoyed frequenting the nightclubs in Lawrence, Kansas. He was known to be a bit of a ladies' man but unfortunately, for a man of Grissom's perverted tastes, merely seducing a woman was not enough.

On the evening of June 18, 1989, 24-year-old Joan Marie Butler
was out with friends in Overland Park, Kansas. Leaving them
during the early morning, she returned to her apartment. The
following morning she was gone, simply vanished.

There was ample evidence that Joan had made it home. However,
it appeared that she'd been surprised by someone in the residence.
Now she was missing, along with her red Chevrolet Corsica.
Further investigation revealed that neighbors had heard a loud
thump coming from Butler's apartment at around 4:30 a.m. The
police also learned that $900 had been withdrawn from her bank
account shortly after her disappearance. A surveillance camera
showed her drawing the money from an ATM machine, a large
bruise clearly visible on her forehead.

On June 25, police officers spotted Butler's car outside an
apartment complex in Lenexa, Kansas. As they watched, a man
approached the vehicle, then fled when he saw the officers. The car
did, however, provide the police with a suspect. Inside were
Richard Grissom's wallet, checkbook and driver's license.

As a search was launched for Grissom, he appeared next at a
Lenexa apartment shared by Christine Rusch and Theresa Brown,
both aged 22. The roommates were last seen at their residence on
June 25, 1989. The following day, Rusch called Brown's employer
and her own to say that neither of them would be coming to work
as they were feeling ill. Neither woman was ever heard from again.

Meanwhile, the massive search for Richard Grissom continued. On
June 28, police found his car outside of an apartment in

Grandview, Kansas. Inside they found jewelry and credit cards belonging to the three missing women, as well as keys to their apartments.

Grissom was eventually tracked to Texas and arrested at Dallas/Fort Worth International Airport as he tried to board a flight. Despite overwhelming evidence against him, he remained adamant that he had done nothing wrong and refused to divulge the location of the bodies.

Nonetheless, DA Paul Morrison was able to build a strong circumstantial case, leading to Grissom's conviction on all counts. He was sentenced to four life terms with no eligibility for parole until 2095.

Grissom is also a suspect in at least two other murders, including that of Terri Maness, who was found dead in her Wichita apartment eleven days before Joan Butler disappeared.

Joan Marie Butler, Christine Rusch, and Theresa Brown have never been found. Grissom steadfastly refuses to reveal why he chose them, how he killed them, or where their bodies are hidden.

Vincent Groves

It was around 5:30 a.m. on a Sunday morning in August 1988, and a Denver, Colorado man was up early, getting ready to compete in a triathlon later that day. As he loaded his gear into his car, another vehicle pulled into the alley behind his Park Hill home. The man peered over his fence and saw a blue car, headlights off. A tall, black man was getting out of it. He couldn't make out the man's face.

The driver nervously opened the car's trunk and lifted out a bundle. The witness at first thought it was trash. To his horror, he realized it was a woman's body. He ran inside to call the police, hearing as he did, a car door slam and an engine start up.

Police officers were soon on the scene. The victim was identified as Pam Montgomery, the latest in a series of prostitute slayings that was already the city's most deadly. And despite investigators early elation at eventually having an eyewitness, the man's testimony proved worthless. He hadn't seen the killer's face, hadn't been able to make out the license plate number. It was typical of the bad luck that had stymied the investigation, allowing the killer to get away with 17 murders thus far.

The first victim was 17-year-old prostitute, Jeanette Baca, found June 11, 1978, in Jefferson County. Less than a month later, the strangled corpse of Joyce Ramey, 23, was found in a field near Stapleton International Airport. Norma Jean Halford, 21, turned up in an abandoned car in Clear Creek County in August 1979.

The following year, Cynthia Boyd, 19, Juanita Mitchell, 25, and Pamela Morgan, 17, were all found beaten and strangled to death, before the killings inexplicably stopped.

Five years passed with no headway in the investigation and no more murders. Then, in April 1987, police were called to a site in Douglas County, where the body of 30-year-old prostitute, Rhonda Fisher, had been discovered.

While investigators pondered this new crime, another prostitute turned up dead. She was 18-year-old Karolyn Walker, discovered in Aurora on July 5, 1987.

And still, the killing continued. Zabra Mason, 19, was found in Lakewood in September 1987; Faye Johnson, 22, turned up in Arapahoe County on January 30, 1988; Juanita Lovato, 19, Diann Mancera, 25, and Carolyn Buchanan, 35, followed. Then there was

Pamela Montgomery. And still, the police were no closer to apprehending the killer.

Then, at last, investigators got a break in the case. Michael Crawford Wilson, an inmate serving time at Ohio State Correctional Facility, contacted the task force and told them about a prisoner he had served time with in Colorado. The man, Vincent Groves, had been convicted of the second-degree murder of a prostitute and had vowed to "roam the streets seeking revenge" when he was released.

As investigators began looking into Groves' background a number of things jumped out at them. The first was that the five-year break in the killings coincided exactly with the period that Groves had been in prison. The second was that Groves was the last person seen with at least five of the slain women. He also knew many of the other victims and had, in fact, lived with two of them.

Groves was brought in for questioning and under interrogation was caught in a series of lies. And when DNA and forensic evidence linked him to several of the victims, police believed they had their man.

Unfortunately, the case was more difficult to prove than they thought. Groves did not deny knowing the women and readily admitted to having sex with several of them. He also admitted that many of the women had driven in his car, accounting for the hair and other forensic evidence found there. None of that made him a killer.

In the end, the DA was able to convict on only two of the murders. Groves was sentenced to life in prison. He died there on October 31, 1996.

Ralph Harris

It is a common misconception that all serial killers suffer childhood abuse and deprivation. This is not so. In fact, some of the most depraved killers, Bundy and Dahmer for example, come from backgrounds that were by all accounts stable and loving. Another such example is Ralph Harris, one of the most ruthless murderers in Chicago's history.

Harris began his criminal career early. In 1989, aged just 17, he stabbed a man with a screwdriver on a Chicago train and stole his jacket. That earned Harris a one-year sentence, but he'd barely been released when he was in trouble again, this time for being found in possession of a concealed handgun. In 1991, he graduated to armed robbery, including among his victims a retired Chicago police sergeant, and an elderly woman and her grandchildren, who he terrorized at gunpoint.

Given his rapid descent into ever more serious crimes, it was only a matter of time before Harris killed someone, and so it proved. From July 1992 to August 1995, he unleashed a campaign of terror against the residents of Chatham, in southeast Chicago. During the course of nine robberies, he shot eleven men, killing six and injuring five, some of them seriously. Not content with murder, he also added rape to his catalog of evil, sexually assaulting six women at gunpoint.

Unlike many serial killers, whose victims fit a certain profile, Harris was indiscriminate in dispensing his unique brand of brutality. He targeted men and women, young and old, their only commonality the misfortune of encountering Ralph Harris.

Even more startling is that although Harris' killing spree extended over a three-year period, for much of that time (August 1992 to January 1995) he was serving a prison term for armed robbery. That means that his spree was confined to just 8 months, during which he murdered, raped, and robbed twenty-six victims.

Between July and August 1992, Harris carried out seven attacks, killing Thomas Hodges, Jimmie Bramlett, David Ford, and William Patterson, seriously injuring Danny Smith, Willie Williams, and James Patterson.

Then, after his period of incarceration, he quickly resumed his murderous activities. Eric Watkins and James Williamson were killed, James Henry and James Brown survived, but with serious physical and emotional scars.

During this latter period, Harris also began sexually assaulting his female victims. Marilyn Edwards, Bettye Webber, Joan Porche, Rhonda Thompson, Rita Jackson, and Deyonous Moore were variously raped, sodomized, and forced to perform oral sex before being robbed of their possessions.

Who knows how many victims Harris would have claimed had Chicago PD detectives not arrested him on August 29, 1995.

He was certainly unrepentant. In fact, he seemed eager to talk about his exploits, proud of what he'd done. Not that it would have made much difference if he'd claimed innocence. The case against him was one of the strongest ever presented in an Illinois courtroom, and included virtually every form of evidence available – eyewitness identification, DNA evidence, ballistics evidence, fingerprint evidence and his own confessions. It was no surprise when the judge eventually announced his guilty verdict and handed down two death sentences plus one hundred and twenty years in prison.

Harris' death sentences were later commuted to life in prison. He will never be released.

Robert Dale Henderson

Robert Dale Henderson was the kind of serial killer who presents an investigative nightmare for homicide detectives, a shiftless rambler who travels from place to place, killing as the mood takes him. By Henderson's own admission he committed 12 murders across Ohio, Louisiana, Arkansas, Mississippi, and Florida. His victims included his wife's parents and brother, plus nine strangers, chosen at random.

How long Henderson might have gone on killing and how many lives he might have claimed, is open to conjecture. However, in a move atypical of serial killers, he surrendered himself to police on February 6, 1982.

Once in custody, Henderson informed Charlotte County officers that he was wanted for murder in several states, including in Putnam County, Florida. The Charlotte officers then contacted their Putnam County colleagues and arranged for Henderson to be transferred there for questioning.

The trip took five hours by car, during which Henderson spoke freely with the two officers escorting him, while avoiding any reference to his crimes. Then, as they arrived at the Putnam

County lock-up, he suddenly changed his tune and announced that he wanted to help with the investigation.

After being advised of his rights, Henderson led investigators to the shallow graves of three of his victims in Hernando County.

The pattern was repeated just months later, while Henderson was being transferred from the Raiford State Prison to Hernando County. On that occasion, the escorting officer showed Henderson a photo of a murder victim and asked him whether he knew the woman. According to later court testimony, Henderson apparently told the officer, "Give me a Pepsi and a pack of Winstons and I'll tell you about this shit." He then launched into a detailed confession of his murder spree.

Henderson claimed that he committed his first murder on January 14, 1982, shooting to death an unnamed woman in Ohio. A week later, he killed his wife's parents and their 11-year-old son at their Ohio farmhouse.

Following those murders, Henderson went on a 19-day killing spree, rampaging through South Carolina, Mississippi, Arkansas, Louisiana, and Florida.

His victims included 23-year-old Francis Dickey, of Batesville, Mississippi; 18-year-old Robert Dawson, of Helena, Arkansas; and 27-year-old Vernon Odom, of Clarksdale, Mississippi.

He murdered a 21-year-old model in Charleston, South Carolina, shot to death a nightclub owner in Baton Rouge, Louisiana, and killed an unnamed woman in Pascagoula, Missouri. On January 25, he shot to death retired doctor, Murray Ferderber, and store clerk, Dorothy Wilkinson, in Palatka, Florida.

But Henderson wasn't done yet. On January 28, he picked up three hitchhikers, two men and a woman, bound them with adhesive tape and shot each of them in the head.

He was arrested on February 6, 1982, after surrendering to a sheriff's deputy in Charlotte County.

At trial, Henderson's defense team tried various tactics to save him from execution. They maintained that the murders were not premeditated, tried to claim self-defense in some of the killings, and eventually tried to have Henderson's confessions quashed.

It was all to no avail. Found guilty in Hernando County, Florida, he was sentenced to death.

Robert Dale Henderson died in the electric chair on April 23, 1993.

Raymont Hopewell

A serial killer was preying on the elderly citizens of Baltimore, raping and robbing and stabbing and strangling his frail victims to death, while the police appeared powerless to stop him.

The first attack occurred in February 1999, when 60-year-old Constance Wills was found strangled to death in her West Baltimore home. An autopsy would reveal that she'd also been raped.

That murder, brutal though it was, looked like an isolated incident until November 30, 2002, when a remarkably similar crime occurred. The victim was 88-year-old Sarah Shannon, bound, raped and then strangled in her bedroom at Greenhill Apartments.

Two more years passed without progress in either murder. Then, on May 27, 2005, police were called to an apartment on North Gilmore Street in Sandtown. Inside they found 78-year-old Sadie Mack, her wrists bound with shoelaces. An autopsy later revealed that the killer had strangled her with his bare hands.

On August 21 that same year, Carlton Crawford, 82, was beaten to death in his Greenspring Avenue home. The killer was surprised at his work when a 31-year-old friend of Crawford's called at the apartment. The man was beaten and robbed, but survived and was able to provide police with a description.

But even as Baltimore PD distributed an identikit of the fiend they were hunting, he killed again, raping and strangling 78-year-old Lydia Wingfield in her home on August 30.

Just two days later, he reappeared, this time varying his M.O. The 63-year-old victim was threatened with a knife, tied up and raped, but inexplicably left alive. Less than a week later, he raped a 55-year-old woman at knifepoint, stabbing her several times. She too survived.

With Baltimore PD now desperately working to stop the killer, he launched one final attack, threatening an 80-year-old man and two women, aged 76 and 67, in their Fernhill Avenue home. All three of the victims were stabbed, but survived their injuries. One of the women would later testify that when she opened her door, there was a young man standing there. "I'm here to kill your husband," he said, before forcing his way inside.

Then on September 20, police finally announced a break in the case, with the arrest of Raymont Hopewell. Initially, Hopewell was charged only with the Crawford murder, but as police looked into his background it emerged that he had known several of his victims. One had been the grandmother of a friend, another had had been a former neighbor of his mother, yet another had known Hopewell since childhood, Hopewell had lived in the same apartment block as another.

As DNA evidence firmed up the case against him, linking him unquestionably to the murder and rape victims, Hopewell quickly sought a deal in order to avoid the death penalty. In exchange, he offered a full confession to his crimes.

As investigators had suspected, most of the victims had allowed him willingly into their houses. On other occasions, he had posed as a deliveryman to gain entry.

Hopewell had spent a great deal of time in his victims' homes, both before and after he killed them. In common with other home-invading serial killers, he often fixed himself something to eat and watched television while the body of his victim lay nearby.

Hopewell would eventually be tried on five counts of murder and a plethora of related charges including rape, attempted murder, and theft. He was sentenced to life in prison without parole on September 12, 2006.

Robert S. James

Robert James must rank as one of the most creative killers in the annals of American crime. Not content with such mundane methods as shooting, stabbing or strangling, James resorted to such inventive devices as auto wrecks, drowning, and rattlesnake bites.

James was born Raymond Lisemba in 1895. His parents were Alabama sharecroppers and James had resigned himself to the life of a cotton picker when he learned that he was the sole beneficiary of his uncle's $4,000 life insurance policy. Flush with his good fortune, he moved to Birmingham, changed his name, and began training as a barber.

In 1921, aged 26, he married Maud Duncan, but she quickly divorced him, citing sadistic cruelty.

James moved to Kansas, opened a barbershop and married again. Things were going well until an angry father arrived at James' place of business wielding a shotgun and accusing James of impregnating his young daughter.

Rather than face up to his responsibilities, James skipped town, abandoning his wife. He turned up next in Fargo, North Dakota, where he bought another barbershop. In 1932, he married a

woman named Winona Wallace, immediately taking out an
insurance policy on her life.

Three months later, James took his new bride to Pike's Peak for a
belated honeymoon. Shortly after they arrived, the couple was
involved in an auto accident during which Mrs. James suffered a
serious head injury. James walked away from the wreck with nary
a scratch. Investigators arriving on the scene noticed a bloody
hammer on the back seat, but paid no attention to it.

Despite her injuries, Winona recovered after two weeks in the
hospital. She'd barely been discharged when James reported a new
tragedy. His wife had drowned in the bathtub he said, offering the
theory that she'd probably still been dizzy from her head wound.

James collected a $14,000 insurance payout and returned soon
after to Alabama, where he married again. His fourth wife,
however, was more savvy than her predecessor. When James
insisted on insuring her life, she divorced him. "People you insure
always die of something strange," she said.

Undeterred by this latest setback, James turned his attention to his
nephew, Cornelius Wright. After taking out an insurance policy on
the young man, James invited him to visit while on leave from the
Navy. He then gave Wright the use of his car, which Wright
promptly drove off a cliff, killing himself. An auto mechanic
testified that the brakes had failed. James collected a large double
indemnity payout and moved to Los Angeles.

Shortly after arriving in California, James bought yet another barbershop and married again. His new bride was an attractive blond manicurist named Mary Busch.

In 1935, James roped in a friend named Charlie Hope to help him dispose of Mary, promising Hope a cut of the insurance money. The plan was to kill Mary with rattlesnake venom and, to this extent, Hope acquired two large specimens.

On the night that they were to carry out the deed, Hope arrived at the James residence to find that James had tied Mary to the kitchen table and was trying to force whiskey down her throat, ostensibly to dull the pain. He then pushed her bare foot into a box containing the snakes and left her there to die.

However, when he and Hope returned to the house later on, Mary was still alive, although bitten and in great pain. James then took her to the bathroom where he drowned her in the tub before throwing her body into a lily pond on the property. He then called the police to report the 'tragedy.'

Detectives sent to investigate the incident speculated that Mary had been bitten by a rattler and had, in shock, fallen into the pond and drowned. The incident was ruled an accident and James once again received a generous payout from his insurers. He might well have gotten away with murder had he not come under suspicion months later for incest.

James had gotten involved in a sexual liaison with his niece and once the illicit relationship was reported, he was hauled in for questioning by the police. Interrogation techniques in those days were somewhat more brutal than they are today and under questioning, James let something slip about Mary's death. Investigators seized on this, and eventually extracted a confession.

Tried for murder, James was found guilty and sentenced to hang. He went to the gallows on May 9, 1942, the last man executed by this method in California. Unfortunately for James, the hanging was poorly done and rather than the swift death the rope normally delivers, it took more than ten minutes for him to die.

Jeremy Bryan Jones

In December 2000, a handsome 27-year-old named Jeremy Jones left Oklahoma on a Greyhound bus. Jones was skipping out on his parole and was also being sought in a rape case there, so he was exceedingly grateful to the woman he'd spent the previous night with. She had provided him with a new identity, that of her son who was currently serving a prison term. Jeremy Jones was now John Paul Chapman.

Unbeknownst to his benefactor, Jones was not the unfortunate victim of police persecution that he claimed to be. He was already a serial killer. Jennifer Judd, Daniel Harris, Dora Oakley, Justin Hutchins, Laura Bible, and Ashley Freeman, had all died at his hands. Over the next four years, aided by police incompetence, he'd kill many more.

Leaving Oklahoma, Jones fled first to Tuscaloosa, Alabama, then to Mobile, where he found construction work with a man named Mark Bentley. Jones lived for a time with the Bentley family but was eventually asked to leave, due to his drug usage. He showed up next in Douglasville, Georgia.

On Halloween night 2002, 38-year-old Tina Mayberry left the popular Gipson's Tavern in Douglasville, and walked towards her car. Moments later, she staggered back into the bar, bleeding profusely. Paramedics were called, but they arrived too late to save Tina, who had been stabbed repeatedly.

Jones was a regular at Gipson's and not long after Mayberry's murder, he hooked up with another bar patron, Vicki Freeman. The two moved in together, but in October 2003, Jones was arrested for exposing himself to his neighbor's 18-year-old daughter. He was fingerprinted after this arrest and spent some anxious moments worrying that his true identity would be exposed.

But the computer returned no match to Jeremy Bryan Jones. He was booked as John Paul Chapman. It was the first of four occasions on which the police failed to pick him up. Had they done so, four lives might have been saved.

In February 2004, 47-year-old mother of three, Katherine Collins, disappeared from her Louisiana home. Her body was discovered in a bayou, some 50 miles away, on Valentine's Day. She'd been raped, stabbed, and beaten to death with a tire iron.

On March 12, 2004, 16-year-old Amanda Greenwell disappeared from Arbor Village, a mobile home park on the outskirts of Douglasville. Her body was found a month later. She'd been stabbed to death.

That same month, Patricia Endres disappeared from the beauty salon she ran in Forsyth County. The cash register and Patricia's purse had been emptied but there were no signs of a struggle. Her body would lay undiscovered until Jones led police to it over a year later.

In September 2004, Jones was back in Mobile, hoping to find construction work in the wake of Hurricane Ivan. On Friday, September 17, he phoned Vicki Freeman back in Georgia. That call was made from the home of Lisa Nichols, a 45-year-old divorcee who lived next door to Jones' former boss, Mark Bentley.

Nichols body was found the following day. She had been raped, shot three times in the head, and then set on fire. But this time, Jones had slipped up. A truck with Oklahoma plates had been spotted outside the Nichols home and as the police questioned neighbors' Mark Bentley told them about John Paul Chapman.

Four days later, Paul Birch, the detective assigned to the case, got a call from Jones, posing as Chapman. Birch kept him on the line while the call was traced and units were dispatched to the scene. Jones was still on the phone when officers arrived to arrest him.

Jones was charged with first-degree murder. But even now, the police failed to learn his true identity. It was only after Jones made a call to his mother from prison that he was eventually caught out.

With his real identity finally revealed, Jeremy Bryan Jones was charged with the murders of Amanda Greenwell, Patricia Endres, and Katherine Collins, in addition to that of Lisa Nichols. The killer soon added other names to the list, claiming 21 victims in a murder spree that spanned 12 years and five states.

Jones went on trial for the murder of Lisa Nichols in November 2005. He was found guilty and currently awaits execution in Alabama.

Lewis Lent

On the morning of January 7, 1994, 12-year-old Rebecca Savarese was walking along a road in Pittsfield, Massachusetts, when a pickup truck stopped beside her. The driver produced a gun, then stepped from the cab and tried to force her into the truck. Feigning dizziness, Rebecca waited until the man loosened his grip on her, then shrugged out of her backpack and ran. The attacker followed for a short distance but gave up the chase when another man appeared.

Rebecca's description of her assailant and her description of the vehicle bore fruit when officers made an arrest on Thursday, January 12, 1995. The suspect was Lewis Lent, Jr., a janitor at a local movie theater. The truck, as it turned out, did not belong to Lent, he'd borrowed it. But he was found in possession of Rebecca's backpack and the gun with which he'd threatened the girl.

If the police believed that they'd apprehended a potential child molester they were soon to realize that the arrest was much more significant than that. Under sustained interrogation, lasting over three days, Lent eventually cracked and admitted to two child murders, one in Massachusetts, the other in New York.

The first murder had occurred on October 22, 1990. The victim was a 12-year-old boy named James Bernardo, who disappeared from a Pittsfield movie theater, the same movie theater that Lewis Lent worked at.

According to Lent's confession, he saw James standing alone outside the theater and used a hunting knife to force him into his car. He drove the boy back to his apartment, where he taped him to a bed, cut off his clothes, and sexually assaulted him.

The next morning, Lent killed James by hanging, which had been his intention all along. He then put the boy's corpse in his car and drove to Newfield, New York. The body would eventually be found there, just a short distance from Lent's childhood home.

On August 18, 1993, Lent killed again. According to Lent, he was visiting his parents in New York, when he decided to go cruising, looking specifically for a child to kill. He encountered 12-year-old Sara Anne Wood riding her bicycle home from church.

Once again using the hunting knife as a threat, he forced Sara into his van. Then he drove her into the Adirondack Mountains where he raped her, before bludgeoning her to death with a tree branch.

He buried her body using tools that he'd brought along for that purpose.

Asked whether he'd been sure she was dead when he buried her, Lent said that he hadn't checked because he didn't like touching dead bodies.

Although Lent drew a map of the area where he claimed to have buried Sara, two massive searches failed to turn up her body. She has never been found.

Having confessed to two brutal murders, Lent clammed up, saying he had no more information to share. The police were not so sure. Lent's M.O. was typical of a serial killer and given the gaps between his confessed crimes, investigators were certain that there must be other victims.

A fifty-man task force (including FBI experts) was established to investigate just that possibility. They turned up a number of child murders with possible links to Lent, including those of Sean Googin, 15; Carry Lynn Nixon, 16; Karolyn Lonczak, 18, Bobby Gutkaiss, 15; and Holly Piirainen, aged 10. In addition, they found evidence in Lent's home that he was constructing a hidden compartment behind a wall, potentially for holding child victims.

Lewis Lent eventually stood trial for the murders of James Bernardo and Sara Anne Wood. He was found guilty and sentenced to two terms of life imprisonment.

Matthew Macon

A serial killer was loose on the streets of Lansing, Michigan, killing at such a ferocious rate that city residents cowered in fear while the police launched a massive effort to apprehend the monster.

The first to die was 76-year-old Ruth Hallman, a neighborhood activist who was found severely beaten in her West Lapeer Street home on July 26, 2007. She died from the injuries two days later, without being able to identify her assailant.

Less than two weeks later on August 7, police officers on patrol in Hunter Park, discovered the body of Deborah Kaye Cooke, 36. She was lying against a tree, naked from the waist down, her face bloodied and beaten.

Only two days passed before the killer struck again, killing 46-year-old Debra Renfors. Renfors had previously worked as a prostitute but was trying to clean up her act and had recently moved into a new home in the Old Town district. She was found indoors. Like the other victims, she'd been beaten to death.

Thus far the killer had murdered three women in the space of three weeks, an almost unprecedented rate. Now, unlikely though it seems, he accelerated, launching three attacks (two of them fatal) over the next three days.

On Monday, August 9, 64-year-old Sandra Eichorn was found dead in her rental property on South Genesee Street.

The following day the Lansing Police Chief announced the formation of a task force that would include the FBI and the Michigan State Police. He'd barely made the broadcast when news came of another attack. This time, the killer forced his way into a home on Jones Street and assaulted the 56-year-old householder. Fortunately, the woman's dog came to her rescue, attacking the man and chasing him off.

Although traumatized, the woman was able to provide the police with a description of her assailant, as well as an insight into his M.O. He'd knocked on her door claiming that he was looking for work, she said. Then, once her back was turned, he'd struck her on the head.

The description provided by the woman would ultimately lead to the arrest of a suspect. Unfortunately, that arrest came too late to save the life of the killer's final victim.

On Wednesday, August 11, investors inspecting a vacant house on Hickory Street were shocked to find a severely injured woman inside. The woman, later identified as 41-year-old Karen Delgado-Yates, was a sometime prostitute who often lived in homeless shelters. She died of her injuries on the way to hospital.

Two weeks after the Delgado-Yates murder, the police finally made an arrest. The suspect was Matthew Emmanuel Macon, a 27-year-old Lansing native, with a long rap sheet that included convictions for sexual assault, breaking and entering, larceny, and car theft. He had been in and out of prison since 2001.

Investigators soon added another murder to the indictment, that of Barbara Jean Tuttle, who had been beaten to death in 2004, during one of Macon's brief periods of freedom. There was also evidence to suggest that Macon may have been involved in a series of vicious sexual assaults committed in 2003.

Macon went on trial in June 2008 and received the maximum penalty allowable under Michigan law, two terms of life imprisonment without the possibility of parole.

Michael Madison

Shaeaun Child had had enough of the foul odors emanating from her neighbor's garage. On July 19, 2013, she phoned in a complaint to the police. A few hours later, two East Cleveland PD officers arrived at the address Child's had provided and approached the ramshackle building. Almost immediately, they picked up the stench of decomposing flesh. Inside, they traced its source.

The corpse was of an African American woman. She was naked and despite the level of putrefaction, there were clear signs of trauma. It was quite obvious that she'd been murdered. Her body was wrapped in plastic sheeting. She would later be identified as 18-year-old Shirellda Terry.

After the patrol officers called it in, crime scene units were dispatched to the scene and a search of the immediate area was launched. Before long, it had uncovered two more bodies.

The first was of Shetisha Sheeley, 28, discovered in an overgrown lot less than two hundred yards from the garage. She was dressed only in a green hoodie, her body wrapped in plastic. The second body was found in the basement of a vacant house, two doors down. Wearing only a leopard print leotard, she was similarly wrapped in plastic. She would eventually be identified as 38-year-old Angela Deskins. Decomposition was so advanced in this case that it was impossible to determine the cause of death.

In the case of the two other victims, however, the medical examiner reported that they had been beaten, and then strangled to death with a ligature. There was also evidence of rape and of possible necrophilia. It appeared that the killer had returned to the bodies several times for his perverted purposes.

While the crime scenes were still being processed, a search was launched for the lessee of the garage, a man named Michael Madison. Later that day, he was tracked to his mother's house, where he surrendered to police after a two-hour standoff.

Looking into Madison's background, police discovered that he was an ex-con, and registered sex offender, who had served four years for the attempted rape of an East Cleveland woman. On that occasion, he'd pulled the woman off the street, dragged her into the backyard of a vacant house and was about to rape her when a police cruiser arrived on the scene. His latest victims had not been so lucky.

Madison was questioned at length about the bodies. He wasn't talking about his own crimes, though. He preferred to talk about his hero, Anthony Sowell, another East Cleveland serial killer. Two years earlier, Sowell (known as the Imperial Avenue Strangler) had raped and strangled eleven women, concealing their bodies in his house, wrapped in plastic. The murders committed by Madison might well have been an attempt to emulate those killings.

Michael Madison was arraigned on three charges of aggravated murder on July 22, 2013, his bail set at $6 million. At the time of writing, he has yet to stand trial, but prosecutors have stated their intention of seeking the death penalty when he does.

Jeffrey Mailhot

Between February 2003 and July 2004, three women were reported missing from the streets of Woonsocket, Rhode Island. Audrey Harris, Christine Dumont, and Stacie Goulet were all prostitutes, working the city's red light district around Arnold Street.

At first, the police did not suspect foul play. But that opinion was to change in July 2004, when an anonymous tipster called the Woonsocket Police department and alerted them to the possibility of a serial killer at work. The caller suggested that investigators speak to Jocelyn Martel, a local hooker currently awaiting trial for drugs offenses.

Martel told a harrowing tale about a man who picked her up for sex, then tried to strangle her in his apartment. She'd escaped by gouging him in the eye, she said. She was convinced that he would have killed her, had she not managed to get free. She provided an address at 221 Cato Street. Detectives following that lead found that a man named Jeffrey S. Mailhot lived there.

Obtaining a photograph of Mailhot from the DMV, the officers placed it in a photo spread, which they presented to Martel. She picked Mailhot out immediately. "That's him," she said. 'That's the man who tried to kill me.'

Yet as police looked into Mailhot's background they were almost certain that Martel had made a mistake. A graduate of Woonsocket High School, Mailhot stood just 5-foot-3. He was a blue-collar worker at a local paper mill and had no criminal record, not even a parking ticket. All who knew him described him as a polite, friendly guy who enjoyed working out at the gym and singing at a local karaoke bar.

The local prostitutes, though, told a different story. Several of them had been picked up by Mailhot, taken back to his apartment and then strangled into unconsciousness. Some, he'd let go voluntarily. Others had kicked and scratched and managed to get away. It was strong enough cause for investigators to bring Mailhot in for questioning.

Initially, Mailhot denied everything, even refusing to acknowledge that he'd ever had sex with a prostitute. Investigators tried another tack. Aware that both of Mailhot's parents had died of cancer, they spoke about the fact that he had been able to pay his final respects, while the families of Harris, Dumont, and Goulet, were frantic with worry, not knowing their whereabouts.

That seemed to get through to Mailhot. Eventually, he admitted to picking up prostitutes. Then he confessed that 'things got out of hand.' Finally, he said, "I don't want this shit inside me anymore. I want to do what I have to, to help the situation."

Over the next 6 hours, Mailhot offered a detailed confession to the three murders. His first victim was Audrey Harris, 33, picked up off a Woonsocket Street in February 2003 and driven back to his apartment. As soon as he closed the door behind her, Mailhot said, he put his hands on her throat and began throttling her. After she collapsed to the floor, he placed a pillow over her face.

When he was sure that Harris was dead, he dragged her to the bathtub and then went to bed and passed out. He'd been drinking heavily that night.

When he woke the next morning, he was surprised to find Harris in the tub as he'd committed the murder in 'some kind of trance.' However, he knew that he had to get rid of the body, so over the next two nights he drove around with it in his trunk, trying to find a suitable dumping ground. When he couldn't find a place, he returned the corpse to his bathtub.

He was unsure of what to do next, but then he remembered an episode of 'The Sopranos,' where a body had been dismembered with a chainsaw. He then drove to a hardware store and purchased an electric saw. Later, he dismembered Harris in the bathtub, then bagged her remains and disposed of them in various dumpsters.

He waited fourteen months before committing his next murder, strangling 42-year-old Christine Dumont and following the same grisly disposal routine.

Mailhot was accelerating now, waiting just two months before attempting to kill Jocelyn Martel. A month later, he struck again, killing Stacie Goulet, a 24-year-old prostitute. Like the previous victims, Goulet was strangled and dismembered, her body parts discarded at several dumpsites.

By Mailhot's own admission, he would have continued killing had he not been caught. Fortunately, an anonymous tip-off and the testimony of an awaiting trial prisoner brought an end to his murderous career.

Jeffrey Mailhot was sentenced to life in prison on February 15, 2006.

Lyndon F. Pace

A decade after the depraved psychopath Carlton Gary terrorized the elderly citizens of Columbus, Georgia, another serial killer was preying on elderly Georgians, this time in Atlanta. Like Gary, this killer attacked his frail victims in their homes, sexually assaulting them and then throttling them to death.

The first murder occurred on August 28, 1988, when the roommate of 86-year-old Lula Bell McAfee returned home to find Ms. McAfee's nude body lying face-down on her bed. A strip of cloth was tightly knotted around her neck and an autopsy would later reveal that she'd been sexually assaulted.

Less than two weeks later, on September 10, 1988, Mattie Mae McLendon, 78 years old, was found lying dead on her bed, covered by a sheet. Although no ligature was found at the scene, it was obvious that she had been strangled. She had also been sexually assaulted.

Five months passed before the deadly strangler returned. On February 4, 1989, the police were called to the home of 79-year-old Johnnie Mae Martin. They found her lying on the bed, naked from the waist down, a shoelace knotted around her throat. Like the other victims, she had been raped.

On March 4, 1989, the brother-in-law of 42-year-old Annie Kate Britt found her lying on her bed. She had been strangled to death with a sock that was still knotted around her neck. The medical examiner later confirmed that she'd been sexually assaulted.

With alarm growing at the spate of attacks, Atlanta PD re-examined the evidence in their possession. They knew that they were hunting a single perpetrator due to the DNA profile lifted from sperm retrieved from each of the victims. They knew that the man entered each of the homes by climbing through a window in the early morning hours. Other than that, they didn't have much.

It seemed inevitable that the killer would strike again. But after the Britt murder, he inexplicably dropped out of sight. It would be three and a half years before he returned.

At around 3:00 a.m. on September 24, 1992, 69-year-old Sarah Grogan woke to a noise and found an intruder in her kitchen. Grogan had a gun and she fired at the man, causing him to flee. She then called the police. A crime scene technician was able to lift a clear set of prints from the kitchen window where the man had entered.

In the early hours of September 30, 1992, Susie Sublett discovered an intruder rifling through her purse in her bedroom. The man threatened to "blow her brains out," but the elderly woman managed to fight him off and flee to a neighbor's house. The neighbor called the police and once again a set of fingerprints was lifted from the scene.

As police processed the prints they got two matches, one to the Grogan crime scene, another to an ex-con named Lyndon Fitzgerald Pace. Within days, Atlanta PD had tracked down Pace and placed him under arrest.

Once in custody Pace agreed to give blood and hair samples. These were sent to the crime lab for processing and returned some surprising results. Pace's DNA profile matched the semen lifted from each of the murder victims. In addition, his pubic hair was a match to evidence from the Britt and Martin crime scenes.

Pace was charged with four counts of capital murder. Although his lawyers fought hard to have the DNA evidence suppressed they were unsuccessful. Found guilty of murder, Lyndon Pace was sentenced to death on March 7, 1996.

David Elliot Penton

Among the most despicable of serial killers are those who target children, but even in that insalubrious company, David Elliot Penton defines a new level of evil. If the jailhouse boasts of this depraved creature are to be believed, he is America's most prolific child killer, responsible for the rapes and murders of as many as 50 children, some as young as 3 years of age.

Penton was born February 9, 1958, in Columbus, Ohio. As is the case with many serial killers, he lacked a male role model in childhood, his father having abandoned the family shortly after David's birth.

After graduating from high school he joined the U.S. Army, where he qualified as a truck mechanic and gained a reputation as an expert marksman and soldier, who superiors described as "highly motivated."

All was not well in his military career, though. In 1980 he was charged with keeping alcohol in his locker and a few months later he was found to have lied about his marital status in order to obtain extra benefits. This transgression saw him demoted from sergeant to specialist.

Where Penton's obsession with children had its genesis is unknown, but he later confessed that while serving in Korea, he often used under-aged prostitutes. According to Penton, this was not because of their youth, but rather because children were less likely to carry sexually transmitted diseases.

Back in the States and stationed at Fort Hood in 1994, Penton was charged with killing his own 2-month-old son, after violently shaking the baby when he would not stop crying. Penton entered a guilty plea to manslaughter and was dishonorably discharged from the Army. While appealing his case, he skipped out on his bail and fled to Texas. He'd remain at large for the next three years, with disastrous results for children up and down the country.

On January 19, 1985, five-year-old Christi Lynn Meeks was abducted while playing outside her mother's apartment in Mesquite, Texas. Christi's brutalized corpse was found floating in Lake Texoma on April 3, 1985.

Less than a year after that gruesome discovery, 9-year old Christie Diane Proctor, disappeared while walking to a friend's house in North Dallas. Christie's body would be found two years later in a field near south Plano.

By that time another east Texas girl, Roxann Hope Reyes, just 3 years old, had been abducted and murdered. Roxann had been playing in the garden of her mother's Garland, Texas, home when she went missing on November 3, 1987. Her body was found near Plano in May 1988.

While the Texas authorities were puzzling over this series of child killings, their Ohio counterparts had a brutal murder of their own to solve, although in this case, the perpetrator was easier to pinpoint.

When the body of 9-year-old Nydra Ross was discovered in a creek bed, police immediately suspected David Penton, a friend of the murdered girl's parents. Penton admitted to knowing the girl, and even to smoking crack with her family. But he vigorously denied killing Nydra.

Despite his claims of innocence, Penton was charged with kidnapping and murder on May 10, 1990. His 1992 trial resulted in a guilty verdict and a life sentence, with eligibility for parole in 2027.

In the meantime, Penton had appeared on the radar of investigators in Texas. They knew that he traveled regularly between Ohio and Texas, and began looking into the possibility that he might have been involved in the Meeks, Proctor, and Reyes murders. Unfortunately, that line of inquiry hit the buffers when the police were unable to place Penton in the Dallas area at the times of the killings.

Penton would probably have gotten away with the Texas murders had he been able to keep his mouth shut. But like most psychopaths, he needed the world to know about his misdeeds. He began shooting his mouth off to fellow inmates in Ohio and his boasts eventually reached the prison authorities. They, in turn, passed the information on to Texas investigators.

Penton soon found himself charged and extradited to Texas. Aware that he was likely to face the death penalty if found guilty, Penton asked for a deal, a guilty plea, in exchange for life in prison.

David Penton is currently an inmate in Ohio, where he continues to publically pronounce his innocence. Privately, though, he is known to boast of killing over fifty children. He remains the prime suspect in child murders committed in Pennsylvania, Arkansas, Alabama, Michigan, Georgia, Indiana, and several other states. Investigators believe that his actual number of victims is between 25 and 30.

Reginald Perkins

Reginald Perkins was a consummate liar, an arch manipulator, and the brutal slayer of at least six women over a 28-year period. Add to that, innumerable rapes, countless robberies, and a plethora of other felonies and you have what amounts to a one-man crime spree. Still, according to Perkins, he never did anything wrong. Even as the needle was been inserted into his arm on the day of his execution, he continued to claim that the state of Texas was "murdering" an innocent man.

Born in Arkansas on April 29, 1955, Perkins was raised in Texas, and later relocated to Cleveland, Ohio. By 1979 he was working as a truck driver in that city when he met Ramola Washington. The couple started dating, and a year later Washington moved out of her sister's home to live with Perkins.

Shortly after these new living arrangements were in effect, Washington asked Perkins to return a set of house keys to her sister, Paulette Nelson. Five days later, having heard nothing from Paulette, Washington went to her house on Sowinski Avenue. She found Paulette, 21, lying on the bed, her face mottled and her throat bearing the signs of strangulation. Her infant daughter lay in bed beside her, unharmed.

Paulette Nelson wasn't the only one to meet her death at Perkins' hands during that period. While Perkins was living with Ramola Washington, he fathered a child by another young woman, named Thelma Morman. Thelma's mother, Jennie, lived in an apartment on East 93rd Street. On a Sunday evening in January 1981, Jennie's family phoned the apartment when she failed to show up for a family card game. When she didn't answer, they became worried and went to check on her. They found Jennie dead in the bedroom with two pillows over her face, a scarf knotted tightly around her neck.

Perkins, meanwhile, was living on East 79th Street, just a few blocks away. On December 11, 1981, he lured 12-year-old Lashelle Thomas into a vacant house, where he beat the girl and tried to rape her. But Lashelle fought so hard and screamed so loudly that a friend came to her rescue and Perkins was forced to let her go. He warned Lashelle that he'd kill her if she told anyone about the attack.

Terrified by his threats, Lashelle said nothing. However, the friend told Lashelle's mother, Jerry Dean Thomas, and she confronted Perkins. A few days later Lashelle arrived home from school to find her mother sitting in a chair, the cord of a hairdryer pulled tightly around her neck.

Perkins was immediately suspected and although the police were certain that he'd strangled all three women they lacked the evidence to prove it. They did, however, have him on the attempted rape and assault of Lashelle Thomas and a conviction, in that case, earned him 6 to 25 years. He was back on the streets in 1987.

Perkins returned to Texas to live with his father and stepmother. On May 6, 1991, Shirley Douglas, 44, and her aunt Hattie Wilson, 79, were strangled to death in their home. Perkins had been dating Wilson's granddaughter.

Two years later, Perkins was arrested on a parole violation and shipped back to Ohio to complete his sentence. He was released in 1996 and once again returned to Texas, where his stepmother, Gertie Mae Perkins, hired him as a truck driver in the family business. She also gave him a mobile home.

On December 4, 2000, ten months after setting her stepson up with a job and a home, Gertie Mae Perkins vanished. That same day, Perkins used his driver's license to pawn her wedding ring and soon found himself under arrest. Under interrogation, he quickly cracked and led police to a parking garage, where Gertie's body was found in the trunk of her car. She'd been beaten and strangled to death.

Perkins was convicted of murder and sentenced to die, a sentence that was carried out by lethal injection on January 22, 2009. He has since been linked by DNA evidence to the murders of Paula

Nelson, Jennie Morman, Jerry Thomas, Hattie Wilson, and Shirley Douglas.

Larme Price

On Friday, March 28, 2003, a man named Larme Price, walked into a police station in Brooklyn, New York, and said he had information about a murder.

The murder he was talking about, was in fact, a series of killings carried out during February and March 2003. Four shopkeepers had been gunned down. According to Price, the killer was a man named "Dog."

The murders began on Saturday, February 8, 2003. John Freddy, a 43-year-old Guyana-native, was drinking coffee at a convenience store in Ozone Park, Queens, before starting his shift at a supermarket across the street.

The store's surveillance camera captured the entire attack. Freddy is approached by a man wearing a dark coat, hooded sweatshirt, and baseball cap. The man raises a gun and fires, before walking casually from the scene.

Just two hours later, Indian immigrant Sukhjit Khajala, 50, was fatally shot in the face at his Brooklyn Minimart. Surveillance footage shows the gunman exchange a few words with Khajala before shooting him, cleaning out the cash register, and walking slowly away. Ballistics would later show that the same .40-caliber revolver had been used in both attacks.

Ukrainian-born laundry manager Albert Kotlyar, 32, was shot to death with the same weapon on March 10, in Bedford-Stuyvesant. Ten days later, at around 10:30 a.m. on March 20, Mohammed Abdul Nasser Ali, 54, was gunned down as he stood in the doorway of his store at the corner of Eastern Parkway and Buffalo Avenue. His cousin, Yakoob Abdul Aldailam, 22, who was behind the counter, was seriously wounded.

Despite the ballistics reports and surveillance footage, investigators had no solid leads in any of the cases until Larme Price contacted them. Detective Tony Viggiani, the officer who had taken Price's statement, did not believe that Price was being totally frank with him.

The following day, Viggiani called Price on his cell phone, ostensibly to clear up some details in his statement. In the midst of that conversation, Price suddenly started crying. "Yeah, it's me," he said. "I'm the guy you're looking for."

While Viggiani kept Price on the line, other officers raced to a location in Crown Heights where they placed Price under arrest.

Once in custody, Price came up with a most unusual motive for the murders. According to him, he'd been so enraged by the 9/11 terrorist attacks that he had decided to take revenge against men of Middle Eastern origin. The only problem with that explanation was that only one of his victims was from the Middle East. The others were from Guyana, India, and Ukraine. It also didn't help his case that he had robbed two of the victims.

Price went on trial for murder in 2004. Given that two of the murders had been committed while carrying out a robbery and that he was also considered a serial killer under New York's penal code, there was a very real chance that he would get the death penalty.

In order to circumvent that possibility, he entered guilty pleas to all four counts, offering in mitigation his PCP addiction and a history of mental illness. He was sentenced to life in prison in February 2004.

Robert Rhoades

From the outside, the rig driven by Robert Ben Rhoades looked like any other. Inside, though, there was a carefully constructed torture chamber, equipped with handcuffs, leashes, whips, an assortment of pins, needles and alligator clips, a collection of dildos, and a horse bridle that he'd shove into his victims' mouths to silence their screams. Rhodes was a sadist and serial killer, a trucker who roamed the country and lured any number of women to a terrible death.

In the early hours of April 1, 1990, Highway Patrolman Mike Miller came across a truck parked on the shoulder of Interstate 10, near Casa Grande, Arizona. The hazard lights were flashing, but as the rig was a danger to oncoming traffic, Miller pulled over intending to tell the driver to move on.

As Miller approached the cab he suddenly stopped, blinked and looked again, barely able to believe his eyes. The back doors were open. Inside, chained to one of the walls, was a naked young woman. The minute she saw the officer, she started shrieking.

Miller drew his weapon. As he did, he saw a man approaching from the front of the vehicle. "It's all right, Officer," he said. "Everything's fine."

Despite the man's cool demeanor, Miller wasn't about to take any chances. He ordered the man to place his hands against the side of the truck, patted him down, and then cuffed him.

The trucker, identified as Robert Ben Rhodes, was taken into custody. In the meanwhile, his victim, Lisa Pennal, went to the hospital for treatment of various welts, cuts, bruises, and abrasions. Once she'd recovered sufficiently from her ordeal, she told investigators what had happened.

Pennal said that Rhoades had picked her up hitchhiking just outside of Phoenix, Arizona. Once on board, he offered her a soft drink, and a short while later she fell asleep in the cab. When she awoke, she was chained and naked. Then Rhoades started raping and torturing her. She wasn't sure how long he had held her captive. It may have been weeks. He had bragged to her that he'd been abducting, torturing, and killing women for fifteen years.

Not long after Rhoades' arrest, Arizona detectives learned that Rhoades was wanted in Texas, for an abduction that closely mirrored Lisa Pennal's. Houston PD officers had raided his apartment and found bondage equipment and bloodied clothing. There was also a set of photographs of a young girl, chained and naked and quite obviously terrified.

It took almost a year to identify the girl in the picture. Her name was Regina Walters, aged 14, and she'd disappeared along with another teenager, Ricky Lee Jones.

When Regina's skeletal remains turned up in a barn in Illinois, Ricky Lee was the main suspect. But as the investigation went on, the police began to believe that he too had met with foul play. Based on evidence found in Rhoades' apartment, it now appeared that he may have killed both Regina and Ricky Lee.

Rhoades, meanwhile, went on trial for the kidnapping of Lisa Pennal and was found guilty. While he was serving time in Arizona, Texas prosecutors approached him with the evidence they intended presenting in the Regina Walters trial. They made it clear that they would be seeking the death penalty.

Faced with the prospect of execution, Rhoades offered a confession to the murder, in exchange for life in prison. Asked about Ricky Lee Jones, he clammed up, knowing the police had no evidence in that case.

The pattern would repeat itself a couple of years later, when Rhoades was conclusively linked to the 1989 murders of newlyweds Patricia Walsh and Scott Zyskowski. Knowing that he was caught out, Rhoades confessed, earning an additional two life sentences.

Investigators are convinced that Robert Ben Rhoades is responsible for many more murders than the three he admitted to. Rhoades, though, isn't talking.

Reinaldo Rivera

Reinaldo Rivera does not easily fit the profile of a serial killer. Indeed, you'd be justified in asking how a seemingly normal, successful and intelligent family man, came to plumb the depths of depravity he did. You are unlikely to find a simple answer.

Rivera was born in Madrid, Spain, on September 13, 1963, the son of a doctor. When he was 7, his family moved to Puerto Rico, where he remained until enlisting in the US Navy at 19. After basic training in Florida, he was posted to San Diego, California. He spent most of the next three years at sea.

Following that assignment, he was sent to Washington D.C. where, from December 1986 to March 1991, he worked for the Joint Chiefs of Staff. He also attended the University of South Carolina, earning a degree in business administration.

In 1993, he married Tammy Lisa Bonnette and over the years that followed fathered two children. Naval postings, meanwhile, took him to Pensacola, Florida, and Corpus Christi, Texas, before he was discharged in September 1995. Rivera next moved his family to Aiken County, South Carolina, where he found work as a tire inspector at a Bridgestone/Firestone plant. It was January 1998. So far, Rivera's life read like a viable rendition of the American dream.

Fast forward two years and we find Rivera in an Augusta, Georgia motel room, hacking at his wrists in a vain attempt to kill himself before the police arrived to arrest him. A week earlier he had lured an 18-year-old to his house, raped her, and then stabbed her three times in the throat. The teenager had escaped and helped the authorities to track him down.

Once in custody, it soon emerged that Reinaldo Rivera, was no novice when it came to sexual assault. At least 30 women came forward to complain that he'd tried to lure them into his car by claiming to represent a modeling agency. And it got much worse than that. As detectives continued to probe, they began to realize that they'd captured a serial killer, a fiend responsible for at least four, and possibly as many as 20, brutal rape-slayings.

Rivera would eventually admit to the murders of 21-year-old Sergeant Marni Glista in September 2000; 17-year-old Tabitha Bosdell in June 2000; Tiffaney Wilson, 17, in December 1999; and Melissa Dingess, 17, in July 1999. He also confessed to the rape and attempted murder of Chrisilee Barton, the victim whose escape had perpetuated his downfall. Rivera would lead police to the previously undiscovered bodies of Bosdell and Wilson.

But investigators did not believe that that was the full extent of his victim count. In fact, they were almost certain that he was the man responsible for 15 unsolved homicides in the area, including a series of prostitute murders committed to between 1987 and 1999. If that was the case, Rivera wasn't talking.

Rivera went on trial in early 2004 and insisted from the outset that he wanted the death penalty for his crimes. The jury was happy to endorse his request and on February 20, 2004, Judge Pickett handed down the sentence of death for the murder of Fort Hood soldier Marni Glista. Rivera also drew several life terms for murder, attempted murder, rape, and sodomy.

Reinaldo Rivera currently awaits execution on Georgia's death row.

Harvey Robinson

On August 9, 1992, the body of 29-year-old Joan Burghardt was discovered in her Allentown, Pennsylvania apartment. Joan, who suffered from a mental illness and required assisted living, had been brutally bludgeoned to death, her killer delivering 37 blows to her head, caving in her skull. She'd also been raped, and judging from the evidence at the scene, the killer had masturbated over her body before fleeing.

Less than a year later, on the morning of June 9, 1993, Charlotte Schmoyer, 15, was delivering the Morning Call newspaper in Allentown, when she mysteriously disappeared. A few hours later, police received an anonymous tip that sent them to a wooded area near the East Side Reservoir. There they found Charlotte's body under a pile of leaves. She'd been stabbed multiple times and her throat had been slashed. An autopsy would later reveal that she'd been raped.

A light blue car had been spotted near the reservoir at the time of Charlotte's disappearance. But while the police were focused on following that clue, the killer had already picked out his next victim.

On June 20, he broke into another Allentown residence, intent on attacking the woman who lived there with her 5-year-old daughter. To his frustration, he found that the woman's boyfriend had stayed over. Moving on to the little girl's bedroom, he throttled the child into unconsciousness before carrying her down to the basement. There, he raped and strangled her, tossing her aside before fleeing the scene. Amazingly, the little girl survived.

A week after that attack, the killer broke into the home of 37-year-old Denise Sam-Cali, a local business owner who he'd been stalking for weeks. He attacked her with a knife, chased her out onto the lawn, and raped her. She might well have been killed had her neighbor not heard the commotion and turned on his porch light, causing the killer to flee.

Denise crawled back inside and was able to call 911. After receiving treatment for her injuries, she gave police a description of her attacker. He was a young white man, she said, about five-foot-seven, muscular, and clean-shaven.

Because Denise Sam-Cali had seen her attacker, the police were afraid that he might return to try and silence her. It gave them an idea. Obtaining permission from Denise and her husband, they placed an officer in the home, hoping that the man would return.

The killer meanwhile had been stalking another victim, just a mile from the Sam-Cali residence. On July 14, he broke into the home of Jessica Jean Fortney, 47, raping and then strangling her to death before making his escape.

This time, though, there'd been a witness. Jessica's 7-year-old granddaughter had seen the entire attack. Her description of the assailant led police to believe that it was the same man who'd attacked Denise Sam-Cali.

The police had by now been keeping up their surveillance on the Sam-Cali residence for two weeks. On July 31, it eventually paid dividends.

At around 1:30 a.m., Officer Brian Lewis was positioned inside the house when he heard the sound of someone breaking in. The officer summoned assistance on the radio, then confronted the burglar as he stepped through into the living room. The man immediately went for the gun tucked into his waistband. After a brief firefight, he fled, leaving behind a trail of blood that suggested he'd either been shot or had cut himself crashing through the glass kitchen door.

The police immediately alerted all hospitals in the area, asking them to report anyone coming in with a bullet wound or serious cuts. It paid off. At around 5:30 a.m., a young man limped into the Lehigh Valley Hospital ER with cuts to his arm and leg. He was immediately arrested. His name was Harvey Miguel Robinson, and he lived close to the sites of all the attacks. He was just 18 years old.

Robinson was brought to trial on July 24, 1994. Found guilty of the rapes and murders of Joan Burghardt, Charlotte Schmoyer, and Jessica Fortney, he was sentenced to death. He currently awaits execution on Pennsylvania's death row, at Graterford.

Richard Rogers

During the early 1990's, the bodies of four middle-aged men were found dumped along roads in Pennsylvania, New York, and New Jersey. Each victim had been stabbed to death and then cut into sections, the sections carefully washed and wrapped tightly in several layers of plastic. The body parts were then discarded at the side of the road, often in waste bins.

The series first came to the attention of police with the murder of Peter Anderson, a 54-year-old investment banker who disappeared in 1991. Anderson had last been seen alive at a Manhattan gay bar called the Townhouse. His dismembered corpse was found at a rest area on the Pennsylvania turnpike. It had been neatly cut into seven sections and wrapped in green plastic bags.

A number of fingerprints were found on the bags, but as the technology for lifting prints from plastic did not exist at the time, it did investigators no good. The trail soon went cold.

On July 10, 1992, Thomas Mulcahy, 57, a business executive from Sudbury, Massachusetts, disappeared. Like Anderson, he'd last been seen at the Townhouse Bar and his dismembered corpse was found at two locations in New Jersey. The body parts were wrapped in green plastic and disposed of in trash containers. Once again, there were prints that the police couldn't use.

Ten months later, on May 10, 1993, a man walking along a rural road in Manchester Township, Pennsylvania, found six bags containing chunks of decomposing flesh. The body turned out to be that of Anthony Marrero, 44, a male prostitute whose usual beat was the Port Authority Bus Terminal in Manhattan.

Just two months later, another body turned up. He was Michael Sakara, a 55-year-old typesetter from Philadelphia. Sakara had last been seen at the Five Oaks, a Manhattan gay bar. The following day his head and arms were found next to Route 9W in Rockland County. His torso and legs were found nine miles north, in Stony Point, New York. All of the sections were wrapped in plastic trash bags.

The day after the gruesome discovery, police got a promising lead. A bartender at the Five Oaks told investigators that Michael Sakara had been drinking with a man on the night of his disappearance. She'd overheard the man mention that he worked as a nurse at St. Vincent's Hospital.

Following up on this lead, the police collected photographs of male nurses from several Manhattan hospitals and showed them to the witness. She thought she recognized a man named Richard Rogers, but couldn't be sure. Rogers worked at Mount Sinai, not St. Vincent's, so the police didn't bother following up.

With no further leads to follow, the case eventually went cold. It remained so until 1999 when a call from Thomas Mulcahy's widow prompted investigators to take another look at the evidence.

In the intervening years, the Toronto Police Department had developed a technique for lifting prints from plastic. The plastic bags were sent there for analysis and returned 33 usable prints.

These linked the murders to a single perpetrator but, other than that, did the police little good, as they could not find a matching set in their system. Undeterred, they sent the prints out to every state, hoping for a match.

It came a year later from Maine. The prints belonged to Richard W. Rogers, the same man who'd been at the Five Oaks with Michael Sakara on the night of his death. Rogers had served time in Maine for murder. The victim, in that case, had been dismembered and wrapped in plastic bags.

Rogers was arrested on May 28, 2001. Tried and found guilty, he was sentenced to two consecutive life terms. He has since been linked to two more murders, one in Florida, and one in New York.

Michael Bruce Ross

Michael Ross was born on July 26, 1959. His mother, Pat, was still in high school when she became pregnant and was forced by her parents into marrying his father, Daniel. The marriage was not a happy one. Pat Ross was an unstable woman, who mentally and physically abused Michael and his four younger siblings. When she was eventually committed to a psychiatric institution, her husband sent the children to live with his family in Bridgeport, Connecticut. It was here, at age 8, that Michael had his first sexual experience. He was raped by his teenaged uncle.

Despite his traumatic upbringing, Michael was a bright child who excelled at school and had a special interest in animal science. It led eventually to his acceptance into Cornell University, to study agricultural economics.

Although popular and socially active at Cornell, Ross was already struggling to deal with his violent sexual urges. Those urges led him to start stalking attractive young women and then to attacking and raping those women. Inevitably, those rapes led to murder.

In May 1981, the body of Dzung Ngoc Tu, 25, was discovered at the bottom of a gorge in Ithaca, New York. At first, it was thought that the young woman had jumped to her death. However, an autopsy revealed that she'd been raped and murdered before being thrown into the ravine by her killer.

Seven months later, on January 5, 1982, 17-year-old Tammy Williams disappeared while walking home from her boyfriend's house in Brooklyn, Connecticut. Her body was found in bushes close by. She'd been raped and strangled.

On March 1, 1982, 16-year-old Paula Perrera left Valley Central High School, early. She was feeling ill that day and decided to thumb a ride to her boyfriend's house. She was never seen alive again. Nearly three weeks later, on March 19, Paula's battered body was discovered in a field off Route 211 in Wallkill, New York, raped, sodomized and strangled.

Shortly after the murder of Paula Perrera, Ross moved to Croton, Ohio, to take up a job at a poultry farm. About a month later, on April 2, 1982, he attacked a pregnant woman in her home. Unbeknown to Ross, the woman was an off-duty police officer, and she managed to fight him off. She immediately reported the attack and Ross was arrested the next day.

Out on bail, he flew back to Connecticut. But even with a court date and possible jail sentence looming, Ross couldn't stop killing. On

June 15, 1982, 23-year-old Deborah Taylor disappeared while walking to a gas station after her car ran out of gas. Her skeletal remains were found four months later, tossed into a ditch at the side of the road.

On November 19, 1983, Robin Stavinsky, 19, disappeared while hitchhiking in Norwich, Connecticut. Her remains were found lying in a field a week later.

On Easter Sunday 1984, fourteen-year-olds April Brunais and Leslie Shelley were on their way home from a movie when they went missing. Their brutalized bodies were found days later.

Two months later, on June 13, 1984, 17-year-old Wendy Baribeault was walking to a convenience store when she was abducted from a busy street in broad daylight. Several witnesses saw a man in a blue Toyota pull Wendy into his car, but unfortunately, a search turned up no trace of her. Wendy's raped and strangled corpse was found several days later.

But this time, the police had a clue. They compiled a list of 3,600 men who owned blue Toyotas and prepared for the arduous task of interviewing them all. As luck would have it, the first name on their list was Michael Ross.

At first, Ross seemed to regard the interview as a game, taunting his interrogators by offering snippets of information and then immediately retracting them. Then, quite unexpectedly, he began talking, confessing to the murders of Baribeault, Brunais, Shelley, Williams, Taylor, and Stavinsky. (For some reason he held back on claiming responsibility for Paula Perrera and Dzung Ngoc Tu. It would be years before he admitted to those killings.)

Michael Ross went on trial in July 1987. Found guilty, he was sentenced to death, the sentence eventually carried out by lethal injection on May 13, 2005. He was the first man executed by the state of Connecticut in 45 years.

Paul F. Runge

Like many serial killers, Paul Runge showed early signs of abnormal psychology. Adopted by Richard and Anita Runge when he was six months old, the boy was just eight when he was expelled from Catholic school. Parents had complained about young Paul harassing their daughters.

But that proved to be just a precursor of what was to come. In 1987, when Runge was 17, he kidnapped a 14-year-old Oak Forest girl and handcuffed her in his father's basement. He then repeatedly raped and tortured the girl, and would likely have killed her had she not been able to wriggle free of her restraints and escape. The girl went straight to the police and Runge was tried, convicted, and sentenced to 7 years in prison.

He was out in 1994 and soon trolling for victims. Only now, he was determined that no one would ever live to testify against him again.

In January 1995, Runge married his pregnant fiancée, Charlene. But even before they tied the knot, the young couple shared a dark secret. On January 3, weeks before their wedding, Charlene had invited a friend, Stacy Frobel, to their apartment. Stobel, 25, had become intoxicated and Charlene had insisted that she sleep over. Sometime during the night, Runge bludgeoned Stobel with a barbell, raped her, and then dismembered and dumped her body.

His bloodlust now aroused, Runge hit on a new scheme for finding victims. He placed a newspaper ad for a housekeeper, luring sisters Dzeneta and Ameal Pasanbegovic, 22 and 20, to his home. The women, who had only recently emigrated from war-torn Bosnia, were raped, murdered, and then dismembered in the bathtub. Their remains ended up in various dumpsters.

Runge's next victim was 30-year-old Dorota Dziubak, killed after Runge arrived at her Northwest Side home in response to an advertisement offering the property for sale.

He played a similar ruse on February 3, 1997. On that day, Runge went to the Northwest Side apartment of Yolanda Gutierrez, claiming he was there to view some exercise equipment she had advertised for sale. Once inside, he overpowered Gutierrez. He then raped her and her 10-year-old daughter, Jessica, and stabbed them both to death. Before leaving, he splashed the two bodies with lighter fluid and set them on fire.

Just a month later, he killed again. Kazimiera Paruch, 43, had offered her Chicago home for sale. Runge gained access by posing as a prospective buyer. He then raped and murdered the woman.

Three months after this latest murder, Runge was picked up on a parole violation and sent back to prison. Then, in 2000, investigators got a DNA match on semen lifted from one of the victims and it was all over for Paul Runge.

With the DNA evidence, plus the testimony of his ex-wife (who had actually participated in the first three murders but had been offered immunity), Runge knew the game was up. In June 2001, he offered a videotaped confession to all seven murders.

Runge stood trial in June 2006, was found guilty and sentenced to death. However, with the state of Illinois currently exercising a moratorium on executions, it remains to be seen whether the sentence will ever be carried out.

George Russell

On Saturday morning, June 23, 1990, a McDonald's employee in Bellevue, Washington spotted the naked body of a young woman beside the dumpsters at the back of the restaurant. He immediately called the police, who were on the scene within minutes.

As officers began looking for clues, the body was removed to the morgue where it was determined that she'd been raped and then bludgeoned to death.

An identification soon followed. The victim was 27-year-old Mary Ann Pohlreich. On the night of her death, she'd been seen at a popular singles bar called Papagayo's Cantina. Her car was still there, suggesting that she might have left with her killer.

On August 9, 1990, a little more than a month after the Pohlreich murder, Carol Ann Beethe spent the evening at another popular Bellevue hangout, The Keg. Carol left the bar at around 2 a.m. She was never seen alive again.

The following morning Carol's 13-year-old daughter discovered her mother's body. She'd suffered horrendous injuries, her face beaten to a pulp, a plastic laundry bag knotted tightly around her throat, the barrel of a shotgun forced into her vagina.

At first, the police insisted that the Pohlreich and Beethe murders were not connected. Perhaps that's what they wanted to believe, rather than the more frightening reality that a sexual psychopath was stalking their quiet little town. The next murder removed all doubt.

On August 30, Andrea Levine, 24, had drinks with friends at the Maple Gardens Restaurant in Kirkland, four miles north of Bellevue. Andrea left the bar early, at around midnight, saying she was tired.

Just before sunrise the following morning, Andrea's landlord spotted a prowler near Andrea's window. The landlord's dog frightened the intruder off and after checking that there were no signs of a break-in, the landlord went back to bed.

Over the next two days, the landlord was surprised not to see Andrea entering or leaving her apartment. Eventually, on September 3, he decided to check on her. He got the shock of his life.

When the police arrived they found Andrea stretched out on the bed, covered by a bloody sheet. The back of her skull had been caved in by a heavy object, and a sex toy had been shoved down her throat. Under the sheet, her body had at least 250 slash marks, extending from her forehead to the soles of her feet. There were no defense wounds, leading investigators to believe that the cuts had been inflicted post-mortem.

Two weeks after the Levine murder, a young black man was arrested while prowling a Bellevue neighborhood. His name was George Russell and he was well known to police due to his lengthy rap sheet, which included numerous arrests for burglary.

Investigators were quick to pick up a link between Russell and the three murder victims. It turned out that he knew all of them, had been seen dancing with Mary Ann Pohlreich on the night of her death, and was known to bear a grudge against Carol Beethe. He'd also been heard making insulting remarks about each of the victims prior to their deaths.

Then a friend of Russell's came forward to tell investigators that Russell had borrowed his pickup truck on the night of the Pohlreich murder. When Russell returned the truck, his friend noticed a number of dark stains on the front seat. Police immediately impounded the truck, removed the upholstery and found bloodstains on the inner padding. The blood was a match to Mary Ann Pohlreich.

The case was strengthened even further when hairs found on Russell's rucksack were scientifically matched to Andrea Levine and sperm from Mary Ann Pohlreich's body was proven by DNA testing to be from George Russell.

Russell would eventually be found guilty on three charges of first-degree murder. As the death penalty was suspended in Washington at the time, he drew the next harshest sentence, three life terms without parole. He is currently an inmate at Washington's notoriously tough Walla Walla Prison.

Kimberly Saenz

Medical serial killers commit murder for a variety of reasons. Harold Shipman killed because he enjoyed the godlike power of life and death he had over his patients; Genene Jones killed because she became addicted to the exhilaration of dealing with "Code Blue" situations; Charles Cullen killed out of frustration with his life, which appeared to be spiraling out of control.

Of those three, Kimberly Saenz most resembles Cullen. The former dialysis nurse had been a cheerleader and a talented softball player at school before she had to drop out when she became pregnant in her senior year. Marrying young, she was by all accounts a good parent. She also qualified as a nurse and was described by one employee as "a compassionate, caring individual who assisted her patients and was well liked."

But then something happened that would turn Kimberly Saenz's life upside down. She became addicted to prescription drugs, most of them pilfered from the hospitals where she worked.

In quick succession, Saenz lost four health care jobs. At the same time, she started to have problems in her marriage, with her husband, Mark, filing for divorce and obtaining a restraining order against her in 2007. She was also arrested for public intoxication and criminal trespass during this time.

Despite these difficulties, Saenz had a new job in August 2007, at the DaVita Dialysis clinic in Lufkin, about 125 miles northeast of Houston, Texas.

In April 2008, a Lufkin fire official wrote anonymously to state health inspectors, suggesting that they investigate the DaVita Clinic due to the unusually high number of paramedic calls being logged from that location, 16 in the first two weeks of April alone.

By the time inspectors arrived a few days later, that number had rocketed to 30 for the month (compared to just two in the previous 15 months). Four patients had died, seven had suffered cardiac problems. It was clear that something was wrong. One of the inspectors soon found a common thread. In 84 percent of the cases, the attending nurse had been Kimberly Saenz.

On April 28, 2008, Saenz arrived for work and was told by her supervisor, Amy Clinton, that she was being taken off her dialysis shift for the day and was required to work as a patient care technician.

Saenz was highly distressed at the news, which meant that she would be cleaning up after patients, rather than giving out medication, as she was used to. She was actually in tears as she went around the wards with her mop and bucket.

At around 6 a.m., patients Marva Rhone and Carolyn Risinger arrived at the clinic for their dialysis treatment. A short while later, two other patients reported something disturbing. They said that they had seen Saenz pour bleach into her bucket, fill a syringe with the caustic liquid, and then inject it into the I.V. lines of Rhone and Risinger.

Although neither of the women went into cardiac arrest, later tests revealed the presence of bleach in their I.V. lines and Saenz was fired from her job.

It would take nearly a year, and a protracted investigation, before she was placed under arrest on April 1, 2009. Saenz was charged with the murders of five patients – Clara Strange, Thelma Metcalf, Garlin Kelley, Cora Bryant, and Opal Few. Investigators speculated that she might have killed at least five more.

Kimberly Saenz went on trial in 2012. She was found guilty on five counts of first-degree murder and sentenced to life imprisonment without eligibility for parole.

Tommy Lynn Sells

Tommy Lynn Sells was born in Oakland, California, on June 28, 1964. He had a twin sister, Tammy Jean, and two more brothers. His mother, Nina, would have three more sons after Tommy.

When Tommy was 18 months old, the family moved to St. Louis, Missouri. There, Tommy and his twin sister both contracted meningitis. Tammy died of the infection. Tommy survived.

Nina Sells appears to have been a particularly bad parent. By age seven, Tommy was drinking alcohol and regularly skipping school. From age eight, he was allowed to regularly spend time with an older man who was later arrested as a pedophile. At 10, he was smoking marijuana, at 13 he crept naked into his grandmother's bed. That same year he tried to rape his mother. At 14, he ran away from home, never to return.

From 1978 to 1999, Sells traveled the country, riding freight trains, hitching, or stealing cars. He supported himself through odd jobs and petty crime. He spent time in a number of prisons.

When exactly he first started killing is unclear. He claims to have killed two men before the age of 17, but the details have never been verified.

The first murders definitely linked to him were those of Ena Court and her four-year-old son, Rory, found bludgeoned to death in their home in 1985.

Another particularly brutal family murder occurred in 1987. Keith Dardeen, his wife Elaine, and their 3-year-old son, Pete, were beaten to death in their Ina, Illinois home. Elaine Dardeen was heavily pregnant at the time, but that did not stop Sells raping her, resulting in her going into premature labor. Sells then battered the newborn to death. The case would remain unsolved for 12 years, until Sells confessed.

Others who fell victim to Sells during this period include a young girl in New Hampshire; a woman and her 3-year-old son killed near Twin Falls, Idaho; a vagrant murdered in a dispute over drugs; a prostitute in Truckee, California, and a female hitchhiker in Oregon.

In 1989, Sells served a 16-month prison term for possession of stolen property. Released a year later, he hit the road again and resumed his killing spree.

In September 1991, he killed Margaret McClain and her daughter, Pamela, in Charleston, West Virginia. Eight months later he attacked and raped a woman who tried to help him when she found him begging on the street. Arrested for that crime he spent another four years in prison.

While inside, Sells married Nora Price and on his release in May 1997, he moved with her to Tennessee. But marriage did nothing to quench Sells' murderous impulses. That same year he strangled 13-year-old Stephanie Mahaney, near Springfield, Missouri.

In February 1998, he bigamously married a 28-year-old divorcee and moved with her to Del Rio, Texas. His new wife was a born-again Christian, and for a time Sells played the dutiful husband. Soon enough though, he'd resumed his murderous road trips.

On one of those trips, in early 1999, he raped and murdered a 32-year-old woman and her 8-year-old daughter. On April 18 that same year, he abducted 9-year-old Mary Bea Perez from a music festival in San Antonio. The girl's raped and strangled body was discovered ten days later. On May 13, he lured 13-year-old Haley McHone to a wooded area in Lexington, Kentucky, where he raped and strangled her. In July, he raped and shot Bobby Lynn Wofford, 14, in Kingfisher, Oklahoma.

Back in Del Rio, Sells had turned his attention to 13-year-old Katy Harris, whose parents attended the same church as him. On December 31, 1999, while Katy's father was away on business, Sells broke into the Harris home and tried to rape Katy. When she resisted, he stabbed her to death and also slashed the throat of a 10-year-old friend, Crystal Harris, who was sleeping over. Crystal survived the attack and was able to identify Sells as her assailant.

Charged with the murder of Katy Harris, Sells was found guilty and sentenced to death. He currently awaits execution on Death Row in Livingston, Texas.

Sebastian Shaw

Sebastian Shaw was born in Vietnam on November 28, 1967. His real name was Chau Quong Ho, but he legally changed it on receiving American citizenship in 1986. Shortly thereafter, Shaw joined the Marines, serving until 1990 when he was discharged for being consistently overweight. He was apparently devastated at being rejected by the military, recording his anger and frustration in his diary.

In July 1991, Shaw again had reason to be angry, on this occasion for being fired from his job at Paragon Cable. This time, though, he decided to vent his anger on another human, choosing as his target Jay Rickbeil, a wheelchair bound 40-year-old man who suffered from cerebral palsy. Breaking into Rickbeil's apartment, Shaw found the disabled man in bed and easily overpowered him. He then slashed the man's throat, severing the main arteries and causing him to bleed to death.

A year later, on July 20, 1992, Shaw had a furious altercation with two co-workers at his new job. The argument left him so mad that he wanted to kill them. He knew however that he would immediately be suspected, so he decided on the next best thing. He decided to pick two victims at random. The two unfortunates that he happened to chance upon were 18-year-old Donna Ferguson, and her boyfriend Todd Rudiger, 29.

On the night of the murders, Shaw broke into the couple's Southeast Portland home and tied them up with electrical and telephone cords. He then raped Ferguson before slashing both of the victims' throats.

Forensic tests on the body of Donna Ferguson showed that she had been sexually assaulted, and swabs taken from the body tested positive for the presence of semen. The crime lab was able to extract a DNA profile from the seminal fluid, but at that point, the state DNA database returned no matches.

On June 1, 1995, a man armed with a handgun forced his way into a Southeast Portland apartment and sexually assaulted the female occupant. The intruder then bound the victim's hands and feet before trying to suffocate her with a pillow. When the woman resisted and started screaming, the intruder fled.

However, he left something behind at the scene. A rape kit performed on the victim produced a semen sample. Sent for DNA analysis it produced a match to that taken from Donna Ferguson.

With renewed emphasis given to the case by this discovery, the police investigation began to focus on one man, Sebastian Shaw. Still, it would take three years of painstaking police work before investigators were ready to make an arrest.

Shaw was taken into custody in February 1998. A court order authorized police to obtain a blood sample and as they'd expected, a DNA match proved that Shaw was the killer they'd been hunting.

Faced with the evidence against him, Shaw struck a deal. In order to avoid the death penalty, he offered a full confession to the Ferguson and Rudiger murders,

as well as the rape and attempted murder of the unnamed woman.

In 2001, another DNA match linked him to the murder of Jay Rickbeil.

Shaw has since been connected to a murder that occurred in Castro Valley, California, in 1994. The victim, 14-year-old Jenny Lin, was found stabbed to death in the bathroom of her home. She was naked and it was believed that Shaw had been attempting to rape her when he was interrupted and panicked.

Sebastian Shaw is currently serving life without parole in an Oregon prison.

Mark Smith

Many serial killers show signs of aberrant behavior early in life. Most often, this takes the form of animal cruelty, fire starting, or a precocious interest in sex. Mark Smith, though, showed signs that were even more worrying than those. Mark was just eight years old when he tried to strangle a female classmate. He was only nine when he stabbed a 6-year-old playmate with a penknife, inflicting more than 20 wounds. The boy survived and Mark was sent for psychiatric evaluation. Posterity does not recall the outcome of those sessions. Whatever therapy was delivered, it did nothing to curb the murderous impulses growing within the boy.

According to Smith's later confession, he committed his first murders while serving with the US Army in Germany. The details of those crimes are not recorded but he claims to have killed 8 women, before finishing his tour and returning to the States. It didn't take him long before he picked up his murderous campaign back home.

At approximately 9:30 p.m. on the evening of January 27, 1970, Jean Bianchi, a 27-year-old mother of two, drove to a Laundromat in McHenry, Illinois. About an hour later, she phoned her husband and told him that the laundry was almost done and that she'd be home soon.

When she failed to return, her husband drove to the Laundromat to look for her. What he found, alarmed him enough to call the police. Jean's laundry was still there, along with a half-written letter to a friend. Her car was still parked outside. She was nowhere to be found.

A frantic search was launched for the missing woman. Three days later, her family's worst fears were realized when her partly clothed body was found lying in a small creek not far from the Laundromat. She'd been beaten so badly that her face was unrecognizable. An autopsy would later reveal that she'd suffered 17 stab wounds to her neck, back, and chest. Sand and grass had been forced down her throat. She'd also been raped.

Exactly four months after the murder of Jean Bianchi, a 17-year-old McHenry West High School senior named Jean Ann Lingenfelter went missing. Jean Ann had been studying for her final exams with a friend. When she failed to return, her father called the police and a search party was organized to look for her.

One of the searchers was Mark Smith, who had escorted Jean Ann to her prom just a few weeks earlier. It was Smith who eventually found the body, washed up on the shore of a small lake.

Jean Ann had been savagely beaten, her nose and jaw broken, her liver lacerated. Her vagina had been violently ripped with the neck of a beer bottle. She'd also been strangled with her own bra.

Shortly after the discovery of Jean Ann's body, the police made an arrest after Smith's efforts to involve himself in the investigation (a trait common to many serial killers) led to him incriminating himself.

Once in custody, he had no problem in admitting to the murder, as well as that of Jean Bianchi, a woman in Arkansas, another in Des Plaines, and eight in Germany.

"It was sort of like the so-called ecstasy of the hunt must be for animals," he explained. "Only I'm just a little bit above the hunt in snatching girls."

Smith was tried and found guilty on two counts of murder in 1971, drawing a sentence of 500 years. He has since come up for parole on a number of occasions. Each time he has been denied.

Andrew Urdailes

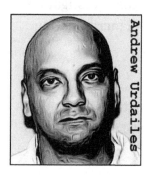

On the evening of Saturday, January 18, 1986, a security guard on the campus of Saddleback College in Mission Viejo, California, spotted something lying on the tarmac in the parking lot. At first, he thought it was a mannequin, some student's idea of a practical joke. But as he got closer and saw the blood on the ground, he realized that this was no prank. He went immediately to call the police.

The victim was identified as Robbin Brandley, a 23-year-old communications major at the college. She'd been stabbed to death in a vicious attack, the killer delivering 41 knife wounds to her neck, back, and chest.

With no evidence left at the scene and no likely suspects, the investigation soon ground to a halt. Meanwhile, the police had their usual roster of homicides to content with. On July 17, 1988,

29-year-old prostitute, Julie McGhee, disappeared from Cathedral City. Her remains were found in the desert days later. Cartridge casings from a .45-caliber handgun were found nearby.

Two months later, on September 25, 1988, another prostitute was killed with a .45. Mary Ann Wells, 31, was found at an industrial complex in San Diego. Not long after, 20-year-old Tammie Erwin was killed with the same .45-caliber weapon.

But even as investigators from Riverside and San Diego counties got together to compare notes, the killer dropped out of sight.

□ □ □ □ □

Six and a half years went by. Then, on March 11, 1995, the .45-caliber killer was back, shooting to death 32-year-old prostitute, Denise Maney. A shell casing left at the scene provided the link.

Just over a year later, a similar murder occurred on the other side of the country in Cook County, Illinois. The victim was Laura Uylaki, a prostitute, who was found in the water at Wolf Lake. She'd been shot twice in the head with a .38-caliber revolver.

On July 14, 1996, the nude body of Cassie Corum, a 21-year-old prostitute, was found floating in the Vermillion River in Livingston County, Illinois. The victim was handcuffed, duct tape binding her ankles and covering her mouth. She'd last been seen leaving a bar in Hammond, Indiana, in the company of a man.

Just over two weeks later, another prostitute, 22-year-old Lynn Huber, was found in the water at Wolf Lake. Like the other victims, she'd been shot in the head.

☐ ☐

On November 14, 1996, a patrolman in Hammond, Indiana, arrested a man named Andrew Urdiales, after finding him in possession of an unlicensed .38 Special revolver. The gun was confiscated and Urdiales was charged with a misdemeanor and released. A few months later he was in trouble again, this time for roughing up a prostitute.

On this occasion, Urdailes was not charged, but investigators noted his previous arrest for the unlicensed .38. They decided to test fire the confiscated revolver and hit paydirt. Ballistics showed that it was the weapon used to kill Laura Uylaki, Cassandra Corum, and Lynn Huber.

☐ ☐

Urdailes was brought in for questioning on April 22, 1997. He initially denied any involvement in the prostitute murders, but then suddenly changed tack and confessed, adding that he'd also killed women in California. The California connection became clear when Urdailes explained that he'd been a Marine, stationed at Camp Pendleton for eight years.

Urdailes went to trial for the murders of Laura Uylaki and Lynn Huber in Cook County, Illinois, in 2002. He was convicted of first-degree murder and sentenced to death, although the penalty was later commuted by outgoing governor George Ryan. The reprieve was short-lived. In 2004, Urdailes stood trial for the murder of Cassie Corum and received another death sentence.

Andrew Urdailes is currently on death row in Illinois. He has yet to stand trial for the murders committed in California.

George Wallace

On December 9, 1990, 18-year-old Ross Alan Ferguson, was approached by a police officer in the parking lot of a grocery store in Van Buren, Arkansas. The officer produced a badge and told Ferguson that he was wanted for questioning in connection with a robbery that had occurred nearby. Despite protesting his innocence, the young man allowed himself to be cuffed and shackled before getting into the back seat of the officer's car.

Once they started driving it became clear to Ferguson that he was not being taken to the police station. Instead, the "policeman" drove him to a remote location in Sebastian County. Once there, he brought the vehicle to a stop beside a pond, got into the back seat and started beating Ferguson.

After several minutes of punching and slapping, he ordered Ferguson from the car and walked him towards the pond. Stopping suddenly, he produced a knife and began stabbing the young man, delivering five deep wounds to his back and one to his arm. Ferguson collapsed to the ground and, realizing it was his only chance of surviving, he decided to play dead. His attacker then dragged him across some rocks, towards the pond. There he removed the shackles and prepared to throw Ferguson into the water.

Seizing his opportunity, Ferguson jumped up and knocked the attacker to the ground. He then sprinted for the car, beating his assailant there. The keys were in the ignition. He started the engine and roared off, leaving the attacker stranded.

Ferguson drove to a nearby house where the residents summoned the police and an ambulance. Officers responding to the call picked up Ferguson's attacker walking in a ditch beside the highway soon after. He was taken into custody and identified himself as George Kent Wallace.

Despite his injuries, Ferguson picked Wallace from a line up. Then after two other young men came forward to testify that they'd also been approached by Wallace, he was charged with kidnapping and attempted murder and held on a $1.5 million bond.

On December 20, with Wallace in police custody, the body of 12-year-old Alonzo Don Cade was found in a gas-well pit near Fort Chaffee. Cade had last been seen alive on November 24, 1990, at a Westark Community College basketball game.

Wallace was questioned in connection with this murder and also about the murder of Mark Anthony McLaughlin, 14, who had gone missing from a Van Buren convenience store on November 11, 1990. He was also interrogated about the murder of William Eric Domer, 15, killed in February 1987. Both boys had been found shot in the head with a .22 pistol, their bodies dumped in a Le Flore County pond.

Wallace had no problem admitting to the murders, even leading detectives to a pasture near Seminole, Oklahoma, where he'd hidden the murder weapon.

Extradited to Oklahoma to stand trial, Wallace insisted that he wanted to die. The judge was only too happy to accede to his request, passing down two death sentences. But once an execution date was set, Wallace had a change of heart and launched a series of appeals. These were ultimately unsuccessful.

George Kent Wallace was executed by lethal injection August 10, 2000. Prior to his death, he confessed to two additional murders, those of Jeffrey Lee Foster in 1976, and Thomas Stewart Reed in 1982. Both murders occurred in Forsyth County, North Carolina, while Wallace was living there.

Thomas Whisenhart

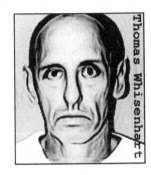

Thomas Whisenhart was born in Mobile, Alabama, on January 29, 1947. His upbringing was highly dysfunctional, with a weak, alcoholic father and a domineering mother who bullied her husband and even physically abused him at times. She nonetheless doted on Thomas, giving in to his every whim and desire and covering for him if he was ever in trouble. She also insisted that he sleep in the same bed with her until he was six years old. He would continue to share his mother's bedroom (but not her bed) until he was sixteen.

According to Whisenhart's sister, Evelyn, Tommy was a normal kid until he was 12 years old. Then something changed. He became moody and aggressive and began hanging out with the local delinquents and getting involved in petty crime. The police, in fact, suspected him in several purse snatchings and minor assaults on young girls, even though he was never formally charged with any of these offenses. Then, one night in 1963 when Thomas was just 16, he graduated to murder.

The victim was a 72-year-old woman who lived across the street from the Whisenharts. She'd been shot with a .32 pistol that had been stolen from a neighborhood home, just days before. The weapon was later found in an empty lot and police bloodhounds led investigators right to the Whisenhart's front door. They suspected Tommy, but his family covered for him, insisting that he'd been home all night.

Whisenhart's next brush with authority came while he was serving in the Air Force. On that occasion, he was arrested for an assault on a woman and was discharged from the service.

Returning to his hometown, Whisenhart married and fathered a child. However, the demons that plagued Thomas Whisenhart would soon surface again, with tragic results for three Alabama women.

On October 16, 1976, after attending a birthday party for his daughter, Whisenhart stopped at a Compact Store in Mobile County where he abducted the clerk, 24-year-old Cheryl Lynn Payton. He drove her to a secluded area where he raped her on the front seat of his pickup truck, then shot her in the head with a .32 pistol. He then dragged Payton's body into nearby woods and left the scene.

But Whisenhart was not done with his victim yet. The following day he returned to her body, this time carrying a knife. Over the next hours, he sat drinking beer and smoking cigarettes beside the corpse. Then he started mutilating it, first cutting off a large section of breast and then slitting open the abdomen.

Unfortunately for Whisenhart, he was observed at the crime scene by a farmer, who called the police.

Whisenhart tried to flee in his pickup. Realizing that he was not going to outrun the pursuing police cruisers, he abandoned the vehicle and ran into the woods. A tense standoff ensued, only ended when officers brought Whisenhart's wife to the scene. Using a loudspeaker, she begged him to give himself up. Whisenhart reportedly yelled back, "I've done everything they said I did." A short while later he surrendered.

Once in custody, Whisenhart readily admitted to murdering Cheryl Lynn Payton, adding that in the previous 18 months he'd committed two more murders, those of convenience store clerks, Venora Hyatt and Patricia Hitt. It was the Payton murder, though, that would eventually earn him a death sentence.

Whisenhart managed to hold out on death row longer than any other inmate in Alabama history. For 32 years 8 months and 20 days he worked the system, raising every appeal and challenge he could. He was 29 years old when he murdered Cheryl Lynn Payton, 63 when he was eventually executed by lethal injection on May 27, 2010. Few killers have deserved it more.

Nicholas Wiley

Two women were dead and one missing from an apartment block in Syracuse, New York, and it didn't take a genius to point out a suspect. Nicholas Wiley, a registered level 3 sex offender, had been released from prison months earlier. He'd only recently been employed as a janitor in the building when the bodies started turning up.

On Monday, June 1, 2004, police officers were summoned to the apartment block by the building manager. He reported a foul odor coming from one of the units, a fact that had been pointed out to him by his janitor. Officers entered the apartment and found the decomposing body of 31-year-old Lottie Thompson. She'd been stabbed to death and had been dead for several days.

As officers cordoned off the scene and began looking for clues, they discovered a second corpse, this one concealed in a dumpster.

She was 22-year-old Hannah Finnerty, another resident of the building. Finnerty had been five months pregnant at the time of her death. Like Lottie Thompson, she died as the result of multiple stab wounds.

Working now on the assumption that the killer may have lived in the apartment building, detectives began looking into the backgrounds of male residents. What they discovered about Nicholas Wiley quickly made them sit up and take notice.

Wiley's turbulent relationship with the legal system began in 1979, when he was just 16. On that occasion, he was convicted of sexually assaulting and stabbing a 25-year-old woman, a crime that earned him four years in a juvenile prison.

He'd barely been released when he was in trouble again. In 1983, he broke into the home of a 67-year-old woman and attacked her with a claw hammer, severely injuring her before making off with $60 in cash and $6 in food stamps. Unfortunately, his initial conviction was overturned on appeal and he was returned to prison on a reduced charge.

Wiley served seven years before securing an early release. He soon reverted to type, attacking a 16-year-old girl, raping and sodomizing her. Convicted of that offense, he served twelve years before his sentence was again reduced on appeal and he walked free.

Now, just five months after his latest period of incarceration, he'd joined the big league. He was the prime suspect in a double homicide.

Wiley was pulled in for questioning on June 2, 2004. After hours of interrogation, he finally admitted to killing Thompson and Finnerty and darkly suggested that there might be other victims.

Looking into that possibility, officers discovered that a third woman, 17-year-old Tammy Passineau, had been reported missing from the apartment block. Passineau's body was never found and authorities believe that Wiley disposed of it in a dumpster and that it was hauled off to the county trash-burning plant.

Wiley would eventually be convicted of all three murders and sentenced to life in prison without the possibility of parole. Meanwhile, the residents of the apartment building on West Onondaga Street were left to wonder why they were never informed about the predator in their midst.

Perhaps Judge Fahey said it best in his summation at the trial, telling Wiley: "You are one of those creatures that occasionally slips through the gates of hell and walks among us causing death, pain, and destruction."

50 More American Serial Killers You've Probably Never Heard Of

Over the course of this series of five books, I've documented the criminal careers of 250 deadly psychopaths who for one reason or another have never achieved the level of infamy of Bundy, Gacy or even someone like Joel Rifkin or Paul John Knowles.

The frightening thing is that these 250 are far from the only ones. It is a sad indictment on our society that these monsters warrant barely a mention outside of local newspapers, that they are processed through the criminal justice system unnoticed to all but the cops who hunt them and the families whose lives they destroy.

In many of these cases, information is difficult to come by. However, I've managed to put together brief summaries of 50 more cases for your perusal. I trust you'll find them interesting.

Franklin Alix: Convicted of shooting to death four people during a six-month killing spree in 1997 and 1998. Alix was executed by lethal injection in Texas.

Paul Bateson: Gay slayer who stabbed to death and dismembered seven men in New York between 1977 and 1978. The body parts were packed in plastic bags and tossed into the Hudson River. Sentenced to life in prison in 1979.

Daniel Joseph Blank: A gambling addiction drove him to bludgeon and stab six people to death in Louisiana between 1996 and 1997. His death sentence was overturned and commuted to life in prison in 2001.

Elroy Chester: Shot five victims to death while committing rape and robbery. Executed by lethal injection in Texas on June 12, 2013.

Scott Cox: A long haul trucker suspected of at least 20 murders across the country, spanning the 80s and 90s. Cox was eventually convicted of two rape-slayings in Oregon. Currently serving a 25-year prison term.

Lawrence Dalton: Raped and murdered four young women in Wisconsin and Illinois between 1977 and 1978. Sentenced to life in prison.

Charles William Davis: A depraved ambulance driver who raped and strangled five women, left their bodies on his route and then called in the crimes himself, so he could go and collect the corpses. Sentenced to life in prison in Maryland in 1976.

Carmello DeJesus: Committed suicide on September 8, 1973, leaving behind a confession to four murders committed in New York, New Jersey, and Florida between 1971 and 1973.

Francisco del Junco: A Cuban immigrant who beat to death and then set on fire four crack addicts in Miami between 1995 and 1996. Sentenced to life in prison.

Frederick Edel: Shot three people to death in 1926 and 1927. Sentenced to life in prison and deported to Germany on parole.

Glennor Engleman: A deadly dentist who supplemented his income by carrying out at least seven murder-for-profit schemes over a 30-year period. Died in prison on March 3, 1999.

Hubert Geralds: Mentally retarded killer who suffered from a compulsion to have sex with women who were unconscious. Claimed five victims in Chicago between 1994 and 1995. Sentenced to death in December 1997.

Waldo Grant: Stabbed, bludgeoned, and dismembered four gay men in New York City, citing an "uncontrollable urge to kill." Sentenced to life in prison in 1976.

Kenneth Granviel: Stabbed to death four women and two children in Tarrant County, Texas, during 1974 and 1975. Executed by lethal injection on February 27, 1996.

Geoffrey Griffin: Known as the "Roseland Killer," Griffin beat and strangled seven drug-addicted prostitutes to death in just two months in 1998. He was sentenced to 100 years in prison.

William Guatney: Known as "Freight Train," Guatney was a rail-riding vagrant who killed at least five (and possibly as many as 15) young boys, aged between 9 and 13. Committed to a mental institution in 1980 and died there in 1997.

Willie Hodges: Brutal rape slayer who sexually assaulted three elderly women, then beat them to death with a hammer. Sentenced to death in Florida in 2009.

Edward Holmes: Lethal pedophile who abducted, stabbed and bludgeoned three children to death in Maryland and Washington DC between September and November 1973.

Philip Husereau: A sadomasochist who beat and strangled to death five of his girlfriends during sex. Died accidently during autoerotic asphyxia on February 18, 1988.

Elton Jackson: Known as the "Hampton Roads Killer," Jackson strangled as many as 12 gay men in Norfolk, Virginia, between 1987 and 1996. Sentenced to life in prison.

Ray Jackson: The "Gilham Park Strangler" raped and strangled six prostitutes in Kansas City, Missouri between 1989 and 1990. Sentenced to six consecutive life terms without parole.

Vickie Dawn Jackson: Nurse who killed at least ten patients by injecting them with a paralyzing drug that stopped their breathing. Sentenced to life in prison in Texas on October 5, 2006.

Sydney Jones: Killed 13 men in random, unprovoked shootings between 1900 and 1914. Hanged for murder in Alabama on June 25, 1915.

Anthony Joe LaRette Jr: Serial rapist who claimed to have stabbed dozens of young women to death. Convicted of three murders and executed by lethal injection in Missouri on November 29, 1995.

Gerald Lewis: Raped and stabbed five women to death across Alabama, Georgia, and Massachusetts. Sentenced to death in Alabama and Georgia. Died in prison on July 25, 2009.

Will Lockett: A rape slayer of the early twentieth century, Lockett murdered three women and a 10-year-old girl. He was executed in Kentucky's electric chair on March 11, 1920.

Neal Long: Racist killer who shot seven black men to death in Dayton, Ohio, between 1972 and 1975. Sentenced to two consecutive terms of life imprisonment.

Richard Macek: Known as the 'Mad Biter' due to the bite marks he left on his victims. Macek raped and mutilated at least two young women and a child. Sentenced to life in prison, he hung himself in his cell on March 2, 1987.

Jerry Marcus: Serial killer and rapist who committed as many as seven murders while drifting between Alabama, Mississippi,

Tennessee, and Georgia. Convicted on only one count, he was sentenced to life in prison in Alabama in 1988.

Joe Roy Metheny: Baltimore area killer of at least ten women. Stabbed his victims to death and mutilated their bodies postmortem. Sentenced to death on November 13, 1998.

Donald Gene Miller: College-educated Miller was a paranoid psychotic and a religious fanatic. Between 1977 and 1978 he raped and murdered four women in and around Lansing, Michigan.

Todd Reed: Claimed three victims in Portland, Oregon, between May and June 1999. All of the women were prostitutes and were raped and strangled to death. Reed was sentenced to life in prison without parole.

Monte Rissel: A brutal rape slayer who claimed five victims by the age of 19. Rissel stabbed and/or drowned his victims. He was sentenced to five life sentences in Virginia in 1978.

Gary Robbins: A traveling salesman who raped, tortured and murdered at least four women across Michigan, Ohio, Maryland, and Pennsylvania during the 1980s. Committed suicide during a shoot-out with police in Pennsylvania on April 14, 1988.

Michael Ronning: Rapist and murderer who claimed seven victims across Arkansas, Michigan, Texas, and Florida, between 1982 and 1986. Sentenced to life in prison without parole.

Brian Kevin Rosenfeld: A deadly nurse who murdered as many as 23 elderly patients in a Florida care home between 1985 and 1990. Convicted of three murders he was sentenced to three terms of life without parole.

Anthony Santo: A triple killer by the tender age of fourteen. Santo was assigned to an asylum for the criminally insane after he stabbed and bludgeoned to death three children in New York and Massachusetts in 1908.

Gary Lee Schaefer: Navy veteran and fundamentalist Christian who raped and beat to death three teenagers between 1979 and 1983. Sentenced to 30 years in a federal penitentiary.

Kenneth Taylor: Thrill killer who cruised the highways and bi-ways of Ohio, Pennsylvania, and Tennessee, gunning down victims at random. Believed to have claimed as many as 17 victims but convicted for only one murder and sentenced to 30 years in prison in 1979.

Joseph Ture: Ax murderer who claimed six victims in Washington County, Minnesota. Sentenced to life in prison on September 23, 1981.

Darryl Turner: Prostitute killer who murdered as many as seven victims in Washington D.C. between 1995 and 1997.

David Villarreal: A homosexual drifter who used a hammer to beat at least seven men to death in Dallas and San Antonio, Texas, between 1974 and 1981.

Frank Walls: Knifed and shot five victims in Okaloosa County, Florida, between 1985 and 1987. Sentenced to death.

Edward Walton: A drifter who shot to death at least five people as he wandered the eastern United States at the turn of the century. The murders occurred between 1896 and 1908. Walton was hanged in West Virginia on July 17, 1908.

Lesley E. Warren: Known as the "Babyface Killer," Warren was a Fort Drum soldier who raped and strangled eight women. Sentenced to death in North Carolina on October 6, 1995.

Richard Paul White: Rapist and torturer White claimed six victims between 2001 and 2003 in Denver, Colorado. Sentenced to three life terms without parole.

George E. Williams: Raped and strangled to death as many as seven Illinois women in 1983 and 1984. Convicted on two counts of first-degree murder, Williams was sentenced to 100 years in prison.

John Williams Jr.: Lethal drifter who stabbed and beat four women to death in Raleigh, North Carolina. Sentenced to death on March 4, 1998.

Leslie Williams: Abducted, raped, and murdered four teenaged girls in southeastern Michigan during 1991 and 1992. Sentenced to life in prison without parole in 1992.

David Franklin Young: A psychopath who beat and stabbed at least three women to death, his murder spree taking in Illinois, Indiana, and Utah. Sentenced to death in 1988.

For more True Crime books by Robert Keller please visit

http://bit.ly/kellerbooks

Made in the USA
Middletown, DE
10 July 2023

34802697R00106